PRIMER contents

CW01085715

PAGE 2
Introduction - A Safe Space
David Shaw
Our editor introduces the issue and articles

Pastor Ian
Please return

PAGE 6
Coming to Terms
Carl Trueman
The Trinity in the early centuries of the church

PAGE 16
God from God, Light from Light
Mark Smith
The eternal generation of the Son

PAGE 26
Something Old - Defending the Title
John James
Basil the Great on the divinity of the Spirit

PAGE 40
Turning Up the Lights
Chris Ansberry
The Trinity in the Old Testament

PAGE 58
Holy, Holy, Holy!
Matt Merker
The Trinity and our corporate worship

PAGE 72
A Profound Mystery
Fred Sanders
How the Trinity helps in our evangelism

a safe space

Introducing the doctrine of the Trinity

You will often hear it said that "Trinity" is not in the Bible, and yet it most definitely is. At the end of Matthew's Gospel we are plainly sent to make disciples and to baptise in the name of the Father, the Son, and the Holy Spirit. One name. A threefold name. Three in one.

And when we witness Jesus' own baptism we get a glimpse of how Father, Son, and Spirit relate to one another and their world. In that glorious scene we hear the Father's delight in his beloved Son who is sent into the world in the power of the Holy Spirit to accomplish our salvation.

The Trinity is in the Bible, and yet, as soon as we let that thought sink in, we realise that we are dealing with profound and mysterious things. The Bible clearly speaks of the Trinity, yes, but the reality it describes - one God eternally existing as three persons - is impossible for us to fully comprehend.

The only proper response, therefore, is humility to receive what God has revealed to us. Of course that means we should not seek to penetrate further into divine mysteries than we can. We are finite creatures and that should never be a cause of resentment. But humility before God will also urge us to go as far as God's revelation allows us to go into these mysteries. To refuse to reflect carefully on what God has said is an act of pride, not humility.

In this task, we can be grateful for the centuries that separate us from Jesus' baptism in the Jordan. It was no small thing to take all that Scripture says about the Father, Son, and Spirit and to find a way of expressing (in creeds and councils) their equality and their eternal relations as Father, Son, and Spirit.

As the church developed its careful expression of those truths it became clear that a major task was to establish the boundaries of a safe space in which we speak of the Trinity. To make it clear what *cannot* be said, and what *must* be maintained if we are going to respect all that God has revealed about himself.

In part, this clearly has a defensive function. False teaching throughout the history of the church has threatened to distort the doctrine of the Trinity. And with dire consequences. If you make the Son a lesser god, a creature, then his claim to reveal the Father is destroyed. God is hidden away. Or if Father, Son, and Spirit are simply roles the one true God has played in history then all we can ever see are the roles and never the actor. God is hidden away again.

And yet, as you can already glimpse, this task of reflecting on the Trinity is also a matter of worship. To discover that we can genuinely encounter the Father, Son, and Spirit in his word and in our hearts is the height of salvation's gifts. We learn to see salvation as a work of Father, Son, and Spirit in which we are caught up into those very relationships. Sons in the Son. Beloved children indwelt by a Spirit through whom the Father and Son come and make their dwelling in us (John 14:23). Which is to say, that in the end, the Trinity is our safe space. Bounded by Father, Son, and Spirit, baptised in their name, we are saved and we are safe. It is glorious to explore these things.

And so to introduce this issue of *Primer*.

First, it is worth remembering that this is the second half of a look at the doctrine of God. In issue o8 we explored God's attributes and the Creator/creature distinction, developing the ways in which our God is wonderfully unlike us. Now we move to thinking about the way in which God exists

Primer issue 08

as three persons and what that means for us. Any understanding of God needs both of these elements. In some ways we have tried to follow the pattern of Scripture itself, in which we meet God first as YHWH, the great "I AM" exalted above his creation, and then in the New Testament we are taught to identify the Son and the Spirit with that God and confess our faith in Father, Son, and Spirit. But that is not to say you have to read issue 08 first! Start here if you like, and then head back to issue 08.

In this issue, Carl Trueman kicks things off with an overview of the early centuries of the church, introducing some of the key figures and debates which set the terms for the doctrine of the Trinity.

Then we have two articles which help us understand the way the Son and the Spirit relate to the Father. The first, by Mark Smith, introduces the doctrine of the eternal generation of the Son, and the wonderful ways in which that eternal truth relates to the sending of the Son in history. The second article features our historical text by Basil the Great. He is indeed great, especially in his defence of the Holy Spirit's right to our worship. John James is your guide to Basil, and he helps us ponder what it looks like to honour the Spirit in church life.

In the next article Chris Ansberry asks how we should read the Old Testament in light of the Trinity. Is the Trinity revealed there in clear ways, hinted at, or hidden until the New Testament? It's a vital question that shapes how we read the Old Testament and how we understand the significance of what God reveals in the ministry of Jesus.

The final two articles dig deeper into the significance of the Trinity for the church's worship and mission. Matt Merker highlights the Trinitarian nature of Christian worship and asks how we can reflect that in the elements of a church service. And then, finally, Fred Sanders asks how the Trinity relates to evangelism. We often think that the Trinity is a mystery that's hard to explain in evangelism. Fred flips it round to suggest the Trinity explains the mystery of evangelism. That's a rather wonderful move and I hope it reinforces a thought that extends across the whole of this issue of *Primer*: the thought that the Trinity is less of a question and more of an answer. Less of a problem, and more of a solution.

DAVID SHAW is the editor of *Primer*. He is a lecturer in New Testament and Greek at Oak Hill College, London, and an elder at Spicer Street Church, St Albans. He's married to Jo and they have four children.

🐦 @_david_shaw

Since there is only one God, why do you speak of three persons, Father, Son, and Holy Spirit?

A. *Because God has so revealed himself in his word that these three distinct persons are the one, true, eternal God.*

Heidelberg Catechism
Q&A 25

The Baptism of Christ
by Jan Swart van Groningen

Coming to Terms

The Trinity in the Early Centuries of the Church

The doctrine of the Trinity is one in which all Christians profess to believe and yet which few of us actually understand. In part, that is inevitable. The doctrine is incomprehensible in the strict sense that nobody can understand God as he understands himself (i.e. infinitely). But it is possible to grasp what the church's doctrinal formulation of the Trinity seeks to safeguard concerning how we speak and think of God's revelation of himself.

CARL TRUEMAN was educated at the Universities of Cambridge and Aberdeen. He is an ordained minister in the Orthodox Presbyterian Church and is currently Professor of Biblical and Religious Studies at Grove City College, Pennsylvania.

For this reason, the doctrine of the Trinity is best approached through the lens of church history. In examining how the doctrine came to be expressed using the language and concepts which the church eventually codified in its authoritative creeds, we can see the concerns which drove those formulations. Most important of all, we can see why alternative formulations were found to be so distinctly inadequate to express the Bible's teaching about who God is.

There is also an aspect of modern evangelical Christian life which obstructs a proper understanding of the Trinity. It is the tendency, perhaps exemplified in Martin Luther's focus on God *for us*, which stresses the content of worship as being that which God has done on behalf of his people. So, for example, we sing of God's amazing grace that "saved a wretch like me" or remind ourselves that before the throne of God above we have a "great high priest whose name is love / who ever lives and pleads for me." Both capture something true and important about the Bible's teaching: God is our God and a God who saves us. But focusing our praise and our teaching on God as he saves, while obviously of great importance, can lead us to neglect praise as contemplation of who God is in himself: the self-sufficient, glorious one who would be glorious even if he had never created this world and saved a people for himself. It is this contemplative aspect of theology, neglected by much of the evangelical tradition, which is underpinned by a robust Trinitarianism and therefore where Trinitarianism becomes practically (i.e. devotionally and liturgically) important.

The Basic Biblical Dynamic

The basic biblical dynamic of Trinitarian theology can be found in two particular strands of New Testament teaching. First, there is the claim (which forms the earliest cry of Christian praise) that Jesus is Lord. Second, there is the baptismal formula which ties together Father, Son, and Holy Spirit in the rite of Christian initiation (Matt 28:19) and thus establishes these three names as essential to the life of the church and her members.

It is important to note the significance of these two aspects of biblical teaching for the later doctrine of the Trinity because they establish at the outset that discussions of the identity of Jesus Christ are intimately connected to the most practical of Christian activities: initiation into the church, and the liturgical praise of the church. While Trinitarian discussion will develop in ways that adopt rarified philosophical language (e.g. terms such as *hypostasis* and *substance*) and concepts (e.g. *simplicity* and *inseparable operations*) the underlying concern of Trinitarian debate could not be more practical: initiation and praise. That in itself should be enough to silence those who would dismiss the Trinitarian debates of the ancient church and their resolution in the fourth and fifth centuries as so much irrelevant intellectual abstraction.

Don't worry - we'll come back to these.

Second, these biblical dynamics focus the issue of the identity of God on the relationship (and thus the respective identities) of the Father and the Son. Historians of the Trinity have often opted for one of two approaches to the subject: they see debates about the incarnation, the identity of the historical Christ, as leading to the formulation of the Trinity; or they see debates about God as Creator framing the discussion and leading to conclusions about the identity of Jesus. It seems that we should not have to choose between these two approaches: the early church was preoccupied both with questions about the identity and significance of the historical Jesus for the identity of the eternal God; and with questions about how God relates to his creation as a means of determining who Jesus was. Both ultimately place the relationship between the Father and the Son, between the Father and the Word at the centre of the question of the identity of God.

Or *Logos*, from the Greek for "word" used in John 1.

The issue of the unity of God – surely one of the most obvious truths which the Old Testament books taught – is deeply challenged by claims that Jesus is Lord and by the baptismal formula. And that makes exploring the identity of Christ in light of the unity of the Creator God to be of paramount theological significance.

The Second Century

The second century witnessed numerous attempts to articulate the relationship between the Father and the Son. In the background were a number of broader doctrinal concerns. Marcion, a native of Pontus who lived in the middle of the century, sought to preserve the unity and indeed purity of God by positing that God was not the Creator but that another, lesser god was the one who created the material universe. Marcion's Christ was connected to the true God and did not possess a material body – matter being something which was corruptible and thus corrupting and therefore not something with which the true God could have direct contact.

In this Marcion appears to have been typical of a number of teachers in the first century who rejected the idea that Christ had a physical body. These are often referred to as *docetics* (from the Greek word meaning 'to seem'). This teaching is found in the Nag Hammadi Papyri, a collection of documents discovered in Egypt just after the Second World War and reflecting the teaching of what scholars now call *Gnosticism*, a word used to categorise forms of early Christianity which lay claim to secret knowledge and which denied Jesus' physicality.

Reactions to Docetism inevitably tended to emphasise the historical, physical reality of Christ's flesh, as we find in the letters of Ignatius of Antioch, an early second-century father. But this only intensified the deeper question of the relationship between the historical Jesus and God and therefore between the Son and the Father. How could worship be given to Jesus, a man, without that constituting idolatry and/or disrupting the biblical teaching on God's unity? Several theologians in the second century offered avenues of explanation.

Justin Martyr (fl. A.D. 160) addressed the matter in a number of his writings where he articulated what is now called 'Logos Christology' which focuses on the divine nature of Christ and therefore has to address how this divine nature is related to that of the Father. To do this, he utilised a number of analogies, most famously that of a torch being lit from a fire: both original fire and torch have the same content – fire – but the lighting of the torch does not diminish the original fire in any way.

'fl.' stands for the Latin word *floruit*, meaning "he/she flourished", and introduces a date during which a person was known to be active.

This approach has a number of things to commend it. First, it is a way of imagining the Father-Son relation which does not reduce the Father in any way, such as, say, the idea of the Son as a branch cut from a tree might do. Second, it emphasises the unity – what we might later call the substantial unity – between the two: in the analogy, Father and Son share fire-ness. Where it falls down, however, is in the way that it allows for the Father to exist independent of and logically prior to the Son. Fire does not carry with it the necessity of lighting a torch. There is a potential logical and even chronological priority of the Father to the Son which would in effect make the Son inferior to the Father.

The second figure is Irenaeus of Lyon (fl. A.D. 180). Irenaeus, reacting to Gnostic and docetic abstractions of Jesus from history, focused very much on the history laid out in the Bible narrative. His thought is very rich and very influential and at its hermeneutical heart lay the notion of *recapitulation*: the Bible story was a unity because historical events in the Old Testament found their counterparts in the New; and the tragedy of the fall found its answer in the work of Christ. Most obviously, as sin entered the world through an historical figure, Adam, so salvation came by an historical figure, Christ. And for this to work, God himself sent his Son to become incarnate and bring creation back into relationship with God. Thus, the Father sent the Son and, with the ascension of the Son at Pentecost, the Spirit continued the work of redemption. Irenaeus is not asking quite the same question as Justin. He is more concerned, we might say, with the *economy* of salvation rather than the *ontology* of the Father and the Son, but he does point to the need to connect ontology and economy in discussion of the Father-Son relationship and offer an historical framework for what will later be Trinitarianism.

It is helpful to distinguish between God's nature in himself and his actions in history. Often this is done with the language of the *economic* Trinity (what we see God doing in time and space) and the *ontological* or the *immanent* Trinity (who God is in eternity).

The third figure is Tertullian (approx. A.D. 150 – 240), a North African layman and the first significant theologian to write in Latin. His contribution came in response to a shadowy figure, Praxeas, who (according to Tertullian) taught that the Father died on the cross. This teaching is a form of what later scholars call *modalism* – a term used to describe a cluster of theologies that see the relationship between the Father and Son as being one of mode of being. Put in very simplistic terms, the Father creates all things and then in some way turns into the Son who is incarnate. This family of heresies has the positive advantage that it gives primary place to the unity of God but falls down because it would seem to require change in God which (among other egregious consequences) jeopardises the notion that the Son can be a revelation of who God is.

By the standards of later Trinitarianism, Tertullian's response is not a particularly adequate one, in that he seems to make God something rather material, akin to a cosmic cloud of some kind. But he does offer a significant development in terms of theological language when he describes God as being one substance but three persons or *personae*. This does not mean quite what person means today in common English usage, but refers to the masks which actors would wear on stage when playing different parts. What is important, however, is that Tertullian here anticipates a vocabulary for maintaining both the unity of the Godhead while also allowing for an account of its multiplicity.

Godhead is often used to refer to the Triune God: "the Godhead" and is capitalised. Or sometimes it refers to the divine nature of God, so we could speak about the godhead of the Son (i.e his divine nature).

The Third Century

Debates in the third century continued to address similar concerns to those found in Tertullian: how was the human Jesus to be understood as special or unique and as the son of God. For example, a theologian called Sabellius presented an argument similar to that of Praxeas, whereby God's unity is maintained by seeing the Son as a mode of God's activity. While this teaching was rejected by the church, it is noteworthy that Sabellius appears to have used the term *homoousios* to describe how the Father and Son are identical with regard to their godhead. That term was codified in the Nicene Creed of A.D. 325 and would later become a vital part of Trinitarian orthodoxy.

A second figure of importance was Paul of Samosata (bishop of Antioch from A.D. 260 until he was deposed in 268). Paul taught that Jesus was unique because he was specially infused with the divine Logos. The similarity with modalism is significant: the unity of God was preserved but at the cost of affirming that the Father and Son were two eternal subsistences in the Godhead.

The single most important theologian of the second century was Origen of Alexandria (A.D. 185-254). Origen was important for developments in biblical interpretation, for defending the faith against pagan criticism and, most important for the doctrine of God, for developing the notion of eternal generation as the way of describing the relationship between the Father and the Son.

Origen's insight was in some senses very simple but also very far-reaching. Two basic ideas lie behind it. First, there is the biblical language of Father and Son. Second, there is the biblical idea that the Son is the image of the Father. The latter point brings out the revelatory aspect of the work of the Son or the Logos: he is a perfect revelation of the Father and therefore must

Homoousios is a Greek term meaning "of the same substance"

From the beginning of the 325 creed:
We believe in one God,
the Father almighty,
maker of all things visible and invisible;
And in one Lord, Jesus Christ, the Son of God,
begotten from the Father, only-begotten,
that is, from the substance of the Father,
God from God, light from light,
true God from true God,
begotten not made,
of one substance (homoousios) with the Father,
through whom all things came into being, things
in heaven and things on earth.

Subsistence refers to a particular being or an individual instance of a particular substance or essence. It is a more accurate translation of the Greek Trinitarian term, *hypostasis* than the more common *person*.

stand in intimate relationship to him. If he does not do so, then he cannot be such a perfect revelation of the Father. And this hinges upon the former relationship, of Father and Son.

For Origen, the biblical language here demanded that the relationship be understood as analogous to that of earthly fathers and sons. Two aspects of this are of particular note. First, to be a father automatically assumes the existence of a child whom one has fathered or generated. Second, given that God is eternal, when the language of fatherhood and sonship is applied to the Godhead, all notions that pertain to time (temporal priority of father over son) must be eliminated. Prior to the birth of my own son, I was not a father; when my son was born, then the language of fatherhood could be legitimately applied to me. But that kind of temporal sequence does not apply to God. The relationship of Father and Son, consistent with God's nature, must be an eternal one. Hence, the importance of the notion of eternal generation: the Father eternally 'begets' – stands in that productive paternal relationship of fatherhood to – the Son.

This represents a distinctly more sophisticated position that either the analogies provided by Justin Martyr or the kind of simplistic emphasis on divine unity we find in Sabellius and (post-Origen) in Paul of Samosata. What Origen is doing is developing a divine ontology – an understanding of who God is in himself in eternity – in order to provide an eternal context for the economy – the actions of God in history. The questions of why Christians baptise in the name of Father, Son, and Holy Spirit, and why they praise Jesus as Lord, can only ultimately be resolved by setting Jesus's identity within the eternal life of God himself. And Origen is key to pointing towards a resolution of that.

There is, however, a small but significant ambiguity in Origen's works. The question of whether the Son necessarily exists or does so simply because God has eternally willed his existence and yet might have chosen not so to do, is left open. That will become very important in the fourth century.

The Fourth Century

The story of the fourth century debates about the Trinity is usually told from the perspective of Athanasius, the great bishop of Alexandria and major protagonist in the controversies of his era. For him, the story was quite simple: Arius, a Libyan presbyter, and his later followers were implacably opposed to orthodoxy and the fourth century is thus a story of a straightforward fight between two sides, the Arians and the orthodox. But this narrative, with its central notion of a heroic Athanasius being at times the lone voice of orthodoxy (often summed up in the phrase *Athanasius contra mundum* – Athanasius against the world) has in recent decades been exposed as far too simplistic. The fourth century was not a straightforward battle between two clearly defined parties; rather it was characterised by a series of theological conflicts and a variety of fluid and shifting theological parties which culminated in the creed formulated at a council in Constantinople in 381, now used by Christians around the world in their worship services and known as the Nicene Creed.

If the narrative of the debates is too complicated to recount in a short article, the basic questions which those debates addressed are not. At heart, the problem of the fourth century is that question of whether the relationship between the Father and Son is a necessary one, or whether the Son can be regarded as somehow dependent upon the will of God, as being (to put it in very crude terms) truly God or merely the first and greatest of all the creatures of God. Athanasius ascribed to Arius a rather crude way of expressing this point: "There was a time when the Son was not" – a statement which clearly made the Father logically and indeed chronologically prior to the Son. If such a statement was allowed to stand, how could they be said to be equal. Further, closely related to this question of the Son's status relative to the Father are two other questions. How can Jesus be considered God if God is unchangeable? And how does Jesus save – or, better, what kind of salvation does Jesus accomplish?

The key to all of these questions was developing a conceptual vocabulary that could be used to describe the relationship between the Father and the Son in such a way that the equality (and unity) of the two was maintained at the same time as the diversity, or distinction between them, could also be expressed. The first council of Nicaea in 325 made some advance in this area. Called to put down the controversy between Alexander, then the bishop of Alexandria, and Arius, the council approved a creedal statement that gave expression both to the notion of eternal generation and utilised the language of homoousios.

Nicaea 325 did not solve the problem, however, but merely set the terms for another half century of debate. The term homoousios – used in the creed of 325 – did

From the beginning of the Nicene Creed:

We believe in one God,
the Father almighty,
maker of heaven and earth,
of all things visible and invisible;

And in one Lord, Jesus Christ,
the only begotten Son of God,
begotten from the Father before all ages,
Light from Light, true God from true God,
begotten not made,
of one substance (homoousios) *with the Father,*
through whom all things came into existence

Notice that, compared to the A.D. 325 version, on page 11 above, this creed is explicit that the Son had no beginning. He was begotten "before all ages."

not emerge as truly significant until mid-century when it became central to attempts to safeguard the equality of Father and Son in terms of their divinity.

It was Athanasius who consistently argued that, if the Son was not as fully God as the Father, and was not one with him, then he could not bring human beings into communion with God. We might recast this by saying that, if the Son was merely like God or was a kind of second-class god, then the incarnation neither truly revealed God nor restored the fellowship between human beings and God. It was in this context that homoousios become a central term, emphasising the unity of substance of Father and Son. An alternative term, *homoiousios*, was proposed by some in the 350s. But, as just noted, *similar* substance means *different* substance and the problems of revelation and salvation remain.

Homoiousios is a Greek term meaning "of *similar* substance." Notice that it is only one letter different to *homoousios* ("of the *same* substance")! One little Greek letter – the iota – makes a massive difference.

This, however, raised other questions: if Father and Son are one substance, what is to prevent them from being like two humans who both possess human substance but are two distinct beings? And does God the Father not change when part of his substance is 'made' into the Son? The language of one substance is not sufficient in itself to safeguard the unity of God and could indeed be used to argue for three gods.

In this context, three further theologians, Gregory of Nyssa, his brother, Basil of Caesarea, and their friend, Gregory of Nazianzus, known collectively as the Cappadocian Fathers, took up the task of refining a second term, *hypostasis* (often translated as 'person'). In 325, the Council of Nicaea had condemned any who claimed that there were three hypostases in God, because at that point in time, hypostasis meant the same as substance. In the 360s and beyond, however, the Cappadocians refined this term to mean something equivalent to subsistence or particular instantiation, while avoiding connotations of substance. It is a fairly refined point: the Father and Son (and eventually in the 370s, the Holy Spirit) came to be described as one substance, three hypostases, with each hypostasis consisting of the whole of the divine substance.

That may sound confusing but what it does is safeguard the biblical teaching and the mystery of the Godhead. The Nicene Creed, as revised and stated at Constantinople in 381, effectively set boundaries to what we can and cannot say about God: we cannot speak about him in any way that denies Father, Son, and Spirit are fully God because that shatters both any notion that the Son reveals the Father or that the Son saves; we cannot speak about him in any way that divides Father, Son, and Holy Spirit up in such a way that each represents a part of the divine substance because that cannot give an adequate account of the Bible's teaching on God's unity; and we cannot collapse the Father and the Son and the Holy Spirit into three temporal modes of the one God because that cannot do justice to the teaching in John's Gospel on the eternal relationship between Father and Son.

Conclusion

Orthodox Trinitarianism is likely to be frustrating when the Christian first encounters it because there is a sense in which it points to how little we can say about the inner being of God. If the Son is eternal, as the Father is, then he must be eternally generated. But that is not to say a whole lot. And if Father and Son are both equally God then they must both be the same substance but not in such a way that their relationship jeopardises divine unity. The Son as Son cannot be less than the Father. He cannot, for example, be subordinate to him, for that would make him less God.

In short, creedal Trinitarianism oftentimes guards us from error by pointing to things we *cannot* say about or ascribe to God. The Trinity is a mystery and as Trinitarianism cuts away inappropriate ways of thinking about God, Father, Son, and Holy Spirit, it reminds us of how finite we are and should drive us to our knees in worshipful – and perhaps silent – contemplation.

Questions for further thought and discussion

One way of creating a safe space for a doctrine of the Trinity is to think about three areas that are off-limits:

1. Look back over the article and try to work out who has strayed outside the safe space and in which direction.

2. Famously, the Trinity has been illustrated in unhelpful ways. How do the following fall down in relation to the diagram?

"Just as water can exist as ice, water, and steam, so God exists in three ways."

"The Trinity is like an egg because you have three things (the yolk, the white, and the shell) in one."

"The Trinity is like one family with three members, like a father and a mother and a son."

God from God, Light from Light

At Christmas, up and down the land, congregations merrily sing:

> *God of God, Light of Light,*
> *Lo! He abhors not the Virgin's womb;*
> *Very God, Begotten not created.*

And yet probably very few stop to think what this slightly archaic-sounding language might really *mean* – let alone how it might express one of the most hard-fought and glorious ideas in the history of doctrine: *the eternal generation of the Son.*

Hard-fought, and glorious; but it is also not easily understood by time-bound creatures. Indeed, Luther went so far as to caution his readers that the topic "is not even comprehensible to the angels." And yet, in the same passage, Luther encourages us to draw near, as far as we can, to a doctrine "given to us in the gospel" and glimpsed "by faith."

In this article, then, we'll explore the limits of what can, and can't, be said about this most central of Trinitarian truths: that the Son of God is eternally begotten of the Father. To do this, we'll begin with some historical background, in order to see how the affirmation of eternal generation became central in the articulation of Nicene orthodoxy; and we'll then consider what the eternal generation of the Son means for us.

Eternal Generation – the heartbeat of orthodoxy

In A.D. 318, a ferocious disagreement arose within the church of Alexandria in Egypt. Bishop Alexander gave an ambitious address to his clergy, in which he emphasised the eternal closeness of relationship (even the co-equality) of God the Son with God the Father. Arius, a clever and remarkably well-read presbyter under Alexander's jurisdiction, immediately accused his venerable bishop of heresy. Alexander's theology, Arius claimed, abolished any meaningful distinction between the Father and the Son, and so ran the risk of advancing either modalism or tritheism. Rather, for Arius,

MARK SMITH is a Fellow of Clare College, Cambridge, where he serves as Dean, and as Director of Studies in Theology. He also lectures in patristics at the University of Cambridge's Divinity Faculty. Mark is married to Phillippa, and they have two daughters.

Martin Luther, 'The Three Symbols or Creeds of the Christian Faith,' in *Luther's Works*, 14:216-218.

Modalism is a view of God as one undifferentiated being, who, like an actor playing different roles in a play, appears sometimes as Father, sometimes as Son, and sometimes as Spirit. By the time of the Arian controversy, any whiff of modalistic doctrine tended to be labelled pejoratively as *Sabellian*, after Sabellius, a shadowy Libyan bishop of the previous century who was believed to have advanced such a position.

Tritheism is a belief in three separate Gods – Father, Son, and Spirit – violating basic biblical monotheism.

> **"**
>
> ...if the Father begat the Son, he that was begotten had a beginning of existence, and from this it is evident that there was a time when the Son was not... that he had his existence from nothing.

Socrates, *Historia Ecclesiastica*, I.5

The conflict spread rapidly, far beyond the bounds of Alexandria, as both Alexander and Arius threw themselves into letter-writing campaigns, seeking to drum up support for their respective causes. Here was a dispute that could not be ignored, still less dismissed as mere theological hairsplitting, the unfortunate by-product of contentious clergy with too much time on their hands. For the clash between Alexander and Arius struck along deep, pre-existing fault lines in the articulation of the church's faith: what did it truly mean for the Father to *be* the Father, and the Son to *be* the Son?

Arius had the more adept publicity machine – he even composed sea-shanties, so that his doctrines could be memorised and spread by sailors (Philostorgius, *Historia Ecclesiastica*, II.2).

This was, in fact, precisely how the Emperor Constantine initially sought to defuse the whole controversy, writing in a letter to Alexander and Arius that the cause was "of a truly insignificant character, and quite unworthy of such fierce argument" but was rather "engendered by the contentious spirit which is fostered by misused leisure." (Eusebius, *Vita Constantini*, II.64f).

Arius saw himself as a simple defender of traditional biblical monotheism. "We acknowledge," he wrote, "one God, alone unbegotten, alone everlasting, alone unbegun, alone true, alone having immortality, alone wise, alone good, alone sovereign: judge, governor, and administrator of all, unalterable and unchangeable, just and good." For Arius, then, there is one God – the Father – who is alone the unoriginated source and first principle of all reality. God's being or essence (that which makes God *God*) is therefore unique, transcendent and indivisible – there is a great gulf fixed between the uncreated God, and the creation he creates. For Arius it is, therefore, unthinkable that God's being can be shared, imparted or communicated in any way – for this would either imply a partitioning of the Godhead (as if God were a cake that could be sliced up), or would imply two equal and eternal self-existent first principles. Both of these options, Arius argued, are philosophically absurd, and biblically unsound.

Arius' *Letter to Alexander* of 320, in: Athanasius, *De Synodis*, 16.

What, then, does Scripture mean when it speaks of the Father "begetting" the Son? Arius answers that the Father "begat an only-begotten Son before eternal times, through whom he has made both the ages and the universe; and begat him not in semblance but in truth; and made him subsist at his own will, unalterable and unchangeable; perfect creature of God." In other words, just as a human father exists prior to his human son, and that human son has his beginning from his human father, so God the Father existed prior to his Son, and chose to create him. *Begotten*, for Arius, is synonymous with *made*. Since the Son cannot share in God the Father's unique and indivisible divine essence, he must be a creation of God, made out of nothing, not by necessity but by an act of the Father's free and loving will. Through his Son (the "firstborn of all creation"), the Father then creates everything else – the Son is the Father's instrument of mediation, the vital bridge between an utterly transcendent God and his contingent creation. The Son does not share in the Father's nature, but is instead a subordinate being. Here, then, is Arius' account of what it means for the Son to be begotten of the Father.

ibid., 16.

Alexander's position was entirely different, but also focussed on the terminology of begetting or generation. If the Father is eternally and unchangeably the Father, Alexander argued, then he can never be without his Son. The Son must therefore participate in the Father's eternity – his generation from the Father is an eternal reality of the Godhead, rather than a creative act of the Father with a beginning in time. The Son does not derive his being *ex nihilo*, but, precisely as Son, fully and uniquely shares in the Father's *own* being: the Son's generation occurs within, not outside, the unitary divine life. Eternal generation, then, was the crux of Alexander's case – it enabled him to affirm the co-equality and co-eternity of Father and Son in a relation of paternity and sonship, without erasing any inter-personal distinctions (the danger of modalism) or asserting two first principles in the Godhead (the danger of tritheism). In articulating his response to Arius, Alexander was able to draw fruitfully upon the legacy of Origen, the greatest theological mind of the previous century, who had begun to develop this understanding of "an eternal and everlasting begetting, as brightness is begotten from light."

That is, out of nothing.

Origen, *De Principiis*, I.2.4.

It was Alexander's account of eternal begetting that won the day when the Council of Nicaea convened in 325. The second article of the Nicene Creed declares belief in:

One Lord Jesus Christ, the Son of God, begotten from the Father, only-begotten, that is, from the substance of the Father [in Greek: *ek tēs ousias tou Patros*], God from God, light from light, true God from true God, begotten not made, of one substance with the Father [*homoousion tō Patri*], through whom all things came to be, both things in the heavens and those on earth.

The Niceno-Constantinopolitan Creed of 381 further emphasised eternal generation, adding that the Son was "begotten from his Father before all the ages."

The Father is eternally Father; the Son was generated out of the being of the Father from eternity. It is God's nature to be generative and fruitful.

Herman Bavinck, *Reformed Dogmatics, Vol. 2. God and Creation,*
ed. John Bolt (Grand Rapids: Baker Academic, 2003), 259.

Notice the centrality of eternal generation. The Son's relation to the Father is explicitly defined in terms of the biblical language of "begotten" and "only-begotten," and then, against Arius' interpretation, the meaning of this language is carefully clarified in two ways. Firstly, since the Father's begetting of the Son is eternal not temporal, "begotten" and "made" are not synonymous– the Son is "begotten *not* made." Secondly, the Son is not begotten *ex nihilo*, but is "from the substance of the Father" – the Son shares in the Father's unique being ('substance') to the full, as "true God from true God." Eternal generation is therefore intrinsic to the coherence of Nicaea's famous affirmation that the Son is "of one substance (*homoousion*) with the Father."

Notice, too, that here the Nicene Creed bears eloquent witness to the necessity of *theological reflection* on Scripture. Athanasius (who was present at Nicaea as a young assistant to Bishop Alexander) later explained that the framers of the Creed had originally intended to use *only* scriptural terminology, but that the whispering and winking Arians had found ways to twist these words in the service of their own nefarious doctrines. The Creed's authors were thus compelled to reach beyond the language of the Bible, to the more technical vocabulary of "substance" (*ousia*), precisely in order to defend and safeguard the witness of Scripture from those who, by perverse misquotation, sought to undermine it. It is a reminder that the Church's developed teaching regarding the eternally begotten and consubstantial Son does not represent a subversion of, addition to, or distraction from Scriptural authority, but is the means of its preservation. The cry of "no creed but the Bible" is one that Arius would have enthusiastically endorsed.

Athanasius, *De Decretis*, 18.4.

Consubstantial here means that the Son is of the same substance as the Father. Both possess God-ness.

Eternal Generation – what is it good for?

From these beginnings, the doctrine of eternal generation continued to play a vital role in the articulation of orthodoxy during the rest of the fourth century. Although there is not space here to consider the contribution of particular church fathers, this is perhaps a good point to pause, and to take stock of how eternal generation performed a central function in wider reflection on the Trinity.

Indeed, in his survey of the period, Lewis Ayres identifies eternal generation as one of three central principles (along with the person/nature distinction, and the inseparable operation of Father, Son, and Spirit) that constituted pro-Nicene theology. *Nicaea and its Legacy: An Approach to Fourth Century Trinitarian Theology* (Oxford: OUP, 2004), 236.

For a succinct recent summary of the key wider functions of the classical doctrine of eternal generation, see: B. Ellis, *Calvin, Classical Trinitarianism, and the Aseity of the Son* (Oxford: OUP, 2012), 69-98.

Firstly, eternal generation shows us how the divine life is one of ***personal distinction***. The Father eternally begets the Son, the Son is eternally begotten of the Father, the Spirit eternally proceeds from the Father and the Son. The three persons *are* their relations. Our relationships are important, but they don't define us – take them away, and we'd still be around. By contrast, to be God is to *be* relational – it is to beget and to be begotten, to breathe and to be breathed. In this way, eternal generation gives us a way of doing justice to God's oneness *and* his threeness, whilst helping to prevent our language from slipping either into modalism or tritheism. In God there is real personal distinction, yet without division or multiplication of the divine life. For Augustine, this was a truth beautifully expressed by Jesus' words in John 5.26: "as the Father has life in himself, so he has granted the Son also to have life in himself." That is to say, self-existent life ("life in himself") is always and eternally possessed by the Son, but possessed distinctly, as an eternal grant of the Father who eternally begets him.

See the helpful analysis of: K. Johnson, 'Eternal Generation in the Trinitarian Theology of Augustine' in: F. Sanders & S. Swain (eds.), *Retrieving Eternal Generation* (Grand Rapids: Zondervan, 2017), 163-79.

Secondly, eternal generation shows us how the divine life is one of ***ordered* distinction**. The Father and the Son are both fully God, but their relation to one another is not reversible or symmetrical: the Son is begotten of the Father, he does not beget; the Father begets the Son, he is not begotten. Or, to use John's language again, the Father grants "life in himself" to the Son, the Son does not grant "life in himself" to the Father. Eternal generation, in other words, gives us a way of doing justice to order or structure (*taxis*) within the Godhead, without undermining the perfect co-equality of the divine persons.

Thirdly, eternal generation shows us how the divine life is **reflected in God's work of redemption**. The way that God reveals himself to us in this world traces the same shape as God's inner life, without reducing the latter to the former. In eternity the Father begets the Son, in time the Father sends the Son for our salvation – the Son's temporal sending is grounded in his eternal sonship and begotten-ness. Or to put it another way, God can be trusted. What we see is what God is. When he comes to us in Christ, he's not play-acting. God's saving work for us is not an afterthought, an add-on, or just another tick-box on his long to-do list – it's in his DNA, it's who he is. The story of salvation is beautiful, because it expresses in space and time the beauty of the eternal divine life.

Conclusion – God from God for us

In the doctrine of eternal generation, we glimpse something of the unfathomable depths of the love of God, of that unceasingly generous 'movement towards' in the divine life that establishes a reality beyond itself. The true and eternal Son, perfect light of perfect light, the sublime radiance of the Father's glory, acts in love to shine forth upon us; the uncreated Son becomes a created son in the womb of his mother, to draw us wayward sons into his perfect Sonship, that what he possesses by nature we might possess by grace; the only-begotten Son of the Father, full of grace and truth, conforms us more and more to his glorious image, until that day when we shall be like him, for we shall see him as he is. Eternal generation is a doctrine to inspire the mind, but also to make the heart sing.

Questions for further thought and discussion

1. Mark writes that "the Father and the Son are both fully God, but their relation to one another is not reversible or symmetrical." In what ways is that true?

2. One of the other ways in which the relationship between the Father and the Son has been discussed concerns the question of obedience. Is the Son eternally generated by the Father and eternally obedient to him? The question has been highly controversial in recent years and gets quite technical. We have produced a guide to the issues which you can find at *PrimerHQ.com* if you want to dig deeper into that question.

ETERNAL GENERATION IN THE BIBLE

In the late 20th and early 21st century the idea of the Son's eternal generation came under fire. For example, Millard Erickson argued that

> ...the concept of eternal generation does not have biblical warrant and does not make sense philosophically... as such, we should eliminate it from theological discussions of the Trinity.

M. Erickson, *Who's Tampering with the Trinity? An Assessment of the Subordination Debate* (Grand Rapids: Kregel, 2009), 251. Likewise, for a time, Wayne Grudem and Bruce Ware argued against the eternal generation of the Son, thinking it lacked biblical support, but have since changed their minds.

More recently, though, there has been a sustained and broad recovery of the doctrine, most notably in the book *Retrieving Eternal Generation* (Grand Rapids: Zondervan, 2017), edited by Fred Sanders and Scott Swain.

One of the marks of that book is that eight chapters are given over to "biblical reasoning." Very often attention has focused on the Greek word *monogenes* which we find in John 1:14, 1:18, 3:16, 3:18, 1 John 4:9. For a long time this word was assumed to mean "only-born," describing the Son as the only-born of God, and so would speak of the Father as the source of the Son. Because the Son is eternal and has no beginning (as John 1:1 says, he is God and was with God in the beginning) theologians therefore spoke of his *eternal begotteness*, or his *eternal generation*.

More recent studies have suggested that *monogenes* might actually mean *one-of-a-kind* and so not speak about the origin of the Son at all, just his uniqueness, but that is debated. In *Retrieving Eternal Generation* there's an article by Charles Irons arguing we should go back to only-begotten, while Don Carson in his essay is unconvinced and argues for one-of-a-kind.

The doctrine of eternal generation has never just rested on those verses from John, however. Throughout the centuries many Christians have read passages like Ps 2:7, Prov 8:32, Mic 5:2 and Heb 1:5 as indications of the Father's eternal begetting of the Son. Again, there are helpful chapters in *Retrieving Eternal Generation* that explore those passages.

Perhaps most clearly, however, there is John 5:26:

John 5:26 ▌ *"For as the Father has life in himself, so he has granted the Son also to have life in himself."*

As Augustine highlights, there is a striking emphasis on the Son's deity – with the Father he has life in himself – but also his *from-the-Father*-ness here:

> " The Father remains life, the Son also remains life; the Father, life in himself, not from the Son; the Son, life in himself, but from the Father. The Son is begotten by the Father to be life in himself; but the Father is life in himself, unbegotten.

Augustine, *Tractates on the Gospel of John* 19.13

Put that together with John 1:1 and we have the beginnings of a very rich description of God. The Father is God. The Son is God. The Father is not the Son and the Son is not the Father. They are distinct. They are also eternally related to one another in one particular way: the Son has life in himself from the Father and that has never not been true. He is eternally begotten.

A similar account can then be added for the Spirit. The Spirit is God, distinct from the Father and the Son and he proceeds from them (that is, he is the Spirit *of God* and the Spirit *of the Son* (see Rom 8:9 and Gal 4:6) and is sent by them into the world (John 14:16, 16:7) in ways that seem to reveal his eternal procession from them).

Historically, there has been some debate over whether the Spirit proceeds from the Father alone or whether the Spirit proceeds from the Father and the Son. This is known as the filioque ('and the Son') clause. Eastern Orthodox churches do not accept that clause, which began to be added to the Nicene Creed in the sixth century, but Protestant and Catholic churches include it in the Nicene Creed: "I believe in the Holy Spirit, the Lord, the giver of life. He proceeds from the Father and the Son."

So, we can put it together like this:

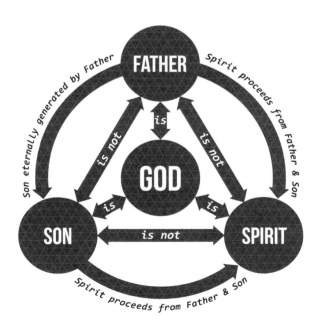

This is an adapted version of a very old way of modelling Trinitarian relationships, often known as the "shield of the Trinity."

DEFENDING THE TITLE

BASIL THE GREAT

VS

THE SPIRIT FIGHTERS

ON THE DIVINITY OF THE SPIRIT

★ FORGOTTEN GOD ★

JOHN JAMES is the pastor of Crossway Church in Birmingham. He is a graduate from Oak Hill College and a trustee of 2020birmingham. His most recent publication is *Together for the City: How Collaborative Church Planting Leads To Citywide Movements*. He is married to Sarah, and they have three children.

"You evangelicals believe in Father, Son and Holy Bible!" Susan muttered to herself, as she left the meeting. It is true that she had previously belonged to a more charismatic church. The music had been livelier, the prayer times more fervent, and the coffee stronger. But none of that annoyed her. She loved her new church, the Bible teaching, the people, and their heart for the community.

It was hard to identify the problem, but somehow the Holy Spirit seemed absent. Perhaps it was the way that he was, or wasn't, spoken of; or the caution around any mention of spiritual gifts; or apparent ambivalence towards his presence and activity. The Holy Spirit was assumed, but never celebrated.

"Well Susan," the pastor had explained, "the Holy Spirit is shy and self-effacing. He has a spotlight ministry on Jesus, so we bring the Spirit glory by bringing glory to Jesus. The Spirit doesn't want us to give him undue attention, and take our eyes off Jesus." Susan had watched enough of *The God Channel* to appreciate the point being made, but still wasn't convinced that *undue* attention was the same as *any* attention.

As sympathetic as Susan was to the pastor's concerns, and as passionate as she was about keeping Jesus at the centre of everything, she still couldn't shake the feeling that the Holy Spirit had, practically speaking, been forgotten.

The scene raises a fundamental question at the heart of Christian piety. How do we honour the Holy Spirit rightly in the life of the church? How do we worship God as Father, Son *and* Holy Spirit?

★ A FOURTH CENTURY WRESTLEMANIA ★

Trinitarian theology has always steered a course between twin dangers. To one side there are heresies which deny that God is eternally three persons, such as modalism, which suggests that the Father, Son and Holy Spirit are successive modes in which the single person of God appears. On the other hand there is polytheism: it is possible to so emphasise the three persons that you effectively make them three gods.

Also referred to as Sabellianism, after Sabellius who promoted this view. See Carl Trueman's article on this.

In light of these dangers, we must say that the Holy Spirit is an eternal person, not the mode of a hidden master. His self-revelation in the economy of salvation is unique, belongs to him alone, and we must relate to him as he is. However, though the Holy Spirit is a distinct person, he remains fully God with the Father and the Son. The Spirit is not a lesser God, or a different type of God. There are not three Gods. We must relate to him as God, and bring him glory with the Father and the Son. The pastor may be right to want to avoid the person of the Spirit eclipsing the Father and the Son, but Susan has a point. We do not worship Father, Son and Holy Bible. Because of who the Spirit is and what he does, he is worthy of equal honour.

The equal honour of the Holy Spirit is not first a contemporary controversy, but an ancient debate. In A.D. 325 the council of Nicaea defended orthodox Christianity against the Arian heresy of *subordinationism*, a belief that the Son was lesser in nature and being than the Father. Nicaea stated firmly that the Son was "of one substance with the Father." This relied heavily on the powerful defence of the Egyptian theologian Athanasius, and his work *On the Incarnation*. It was not long, however, before a similar argument, teetering towards polytheism, sought to demote the Holy Spirit. Athanasius did another sterling job in his letters to Serapion, but a second heavyweight wrestler was required to take on the heretics. Enter Basil the Great.

The letters of Athanasius to Serapion concerning the Holy Spirit were written between A.D. 358 and 360.

Name: Basil
AKA: Basil the Great; Basil of Caesarea
Born: 330
Died: 379

Fact: One of three church Fathers in Cappadocia, modern-day Turkey, who along with his younger brother Gregory of Nyssa and their close friend Gregory of Nazianzus did a great deal to defend the biblical doctrine of the Trinity.

BASIL THE GREAT

The heretics in question were nicknamed the *Pneumatomachi*: "the Spirit-fighters" or "the-fighters-against-the-Spirit." Their position can be reconstructed from Basil's response. They argued that the Spirit must not be ranked with the Father or the Son, because "he is different in nature and inferior in dignity to them." The difference of nature divides the Spirit from the Father and the Son. As a result, though his status may be elevated, the Spirit is not divine, but a creature.

Basil, *On the Holy Spirit*, 10:24.

How does Basil realise there is a problem? He detects it from their *worship*. He notes,

Basil, *On the Holy Spirit*, 1:3.

> Lately while I pray with the people, we sometimes finish the doxology to God the Father with the form "Glory to the Father *with* the Son, *together with* the Holy Spirit," and at other times we use "Glory to the Father *through* the Son *in* the Holy Spirit." Some of those present accuse us of using strange and mutually contradictory terms.

The *Pneumatomachi* are happy to bring glory to the Father "*in* the Holy Spirit," but not "*together with* the Holy Spirit." They might argue that the Holy Spirit is someone special who helps us to approach God, but must not be elevated to the place of God. They say that to pray both doxologies is "contradictory," and gives undue honour to a person who does not seek the attention.

The truth is that these two doxologies, taken together, beautifully reflect Trinitarian orthodoxy. They uphold the distinct relations within the Trinity in a way that affirms their inseparable operation and unity of mission ("Glory to the Father, through the Son, in the Holy Spirit"). And yet also uphold their shared divine essence ("Glory to the Father, with the Son, together with the Holy Spirit"). And they do both in the context of worship.

Basil wrote his work *On the Holy Spirit* between 373 and 375. He died in 379, just two years before the Constantinopolitan council revised the Nicene Creed. It is very possible, though, that Amphilochius, to whom Basil wrote *On the Holy Spirit*, was present at the council and represented his argument. Certainly, the final statement has Basil's fingerprints all over it. The Nicene-Constantinopolitan creed states:

> [We believe] in the Holy Spirit, the Lord and life-giver, who proceeds from the Father, who is worshipped and glorified together with the Father and the Son.

Basil makes his argument in three stages. The first argues that the Spirit is ontologically equal with the Father and the Son. The second stage argues that the Spirit does God's work. He operates inseparably with the Father and the Son in the economy of creation and salvation. The third stage reaches the conclusion that the Spirit is therefore of equal divine essence and so worthy of equal honour with the Father and the Son. The text below is an abridged version of *On The Holy Spirit* that displays some of the key wrestling moves that defeated the *Pneumatomachi*.

ST BASIL THE GREAT
★ ON THE HOLY SPIRIT ★

STAGE 1: THE SPIRIT'S EQUALITY WITH THE FATHER AND THE SON ON THE BASIS OF HIS NAME AND TITLES. [FROM CH'S 9-10]

The first stage of Basil's argument is to consider who the Spirit is. If we consider how he is talked about or addressed within Scripture, it will give us an insight into the nature of his being: his ontology.

Let us now investigate what are our common conceptions concerning the Spirit, as well those which have been gathered by us from Holy Scripture concerning the Spirit, and those which we have received from the unwritten tradition of the Fathers. First of all we ask, who on hearing the titles of the Spirit is not lifted up in soul, who does not raise his thoughts to contemplate the supreme nature? He is called "Spirit of God," "the Spirit of truth who goes out from the Father," "right Spirit," "a leading Spirit." His first and most proper title is "Holy Spirit;" which is a name specially appropriate to everything that is incorporeal, purely immaterial, and indivisible. So our Lord, when teaching the woman who thought God had to be worshipped in particular places said "God is spirit."

John 15:26

John 4:24

On our hearing, then, of this word "spirit," it is impossible to form the idea of a limited nature, subject to change and variation, or at all like the creature. We are compelled to advance in our conceptions to the highest, and to think of an intelligent being, in power infinite, in greatness unlimited, unmeasured by times or ages, generous of his good gifts, to whom turn all things needing sanctification, after whom reach all things that live in virtue, as being watered by his inspiration and helped on toward their natural and proper end; perfecting all other things, but himself lacking in nothing; living not as needing restoration, but as Supplier of life; not growing by additions; but straightway full, self-established, omnipresent, the source of sanctification, light perceptible to the mind, supplying, as it were, illumination to every faculty in the search for truth.

Impassible means that God cannot change or grow in his experience of emotions or passions because he is eternal and perfect. For more on that idea, see Chris Stead's article in *Primer* issue 08.

By nature unapproachable, apprehended only by reason of his goodness, filling all things with his power, but communicated only to the worthy; not shared in one measure, but distributing his energy according to "the proportion of faith;" in being he is simple, in powers various, wholly present in each and being wholly everywhere; distributed, but impassible, he is shared and yet remains whole. Consider the sunbeam, whose kindly light falls on him who enjoys it as though it shone for him alone, yet illumines land and sea and mingles with the air. So, too, is the Spirit to everyone who receives him, as though given to him alone, and yet he sends forth grace sufficient and full for all mankind, and is enjoyed by all who share him, according to the capacity, not of his power, but of their nature...

But now we must proceed to attack our opponents, in the endeavour to refute those oppositions advanced against us which are derived from knowledge falsely so-called.

It is not permissible, they assert, for the Holy Spirit to be ranked with the Father and Son, on account of the difference of his nature and the inferiority of his dignity. Against them it is right to reply in the words of the apostles, "We ought to obey God rather than men." For if our Lord, when establishing the baptism of salvation, charged his disciples to baptise all nations in the name "of the Father and of the Son and of the Holy Spirit." He did not disdain fellowship with him, but these men allege that we must not rank him with the Father and the Son. Is it not clear that they openly reject the commandment of God? If they deny that association of these three names is declaratory of any fellowship and conjunction, let them tell us why we are required to hold this opinion, and what better suggestion they have. If the Lord did not indeed unite the Spirit with the Father and himself in baptism, then let them lay the blame for inventing it upon us. But if, on the contrary, the Spirit is there united with the Father and the Son (and no one is so shameless as to say anything else) then do not let them lay blame on us for following the words of Scripture.

Acts 5:29

Matt 28:19. The baptismal formula is a key argument for Basil in order to rank the Spirit with the Father and the Son, and therefore to consider him equal in being. If the Spirit is honoured with the Father and the Son in baptism, it is because he has an equal and inseparable role with the Father and the Son in salvation.

But all the apparatus of war has been got ready against us; every intellectual missile is aimed at us; and now blasphemers' tongues shoot and hit and hit again, harder than Stephen of old was smitten by the killers of the Christ. And do not let them succeed in concealing the fact that, while their attack is directed against us, the real purpose of these proceedings is much worse. It is against us, they say, that they are preparing their engines and their snares; against us that they are shouting to one another, according to each one's strength or cunning, to come on. But the object of attack is faith itself. The one aim of the whole band of opponents and enemies of "sound doctrine" is to shake down the foundation of the faith of Christ by levelling apostolic tradition to the ground, and utterly destroying it. So, like debtors who refuse to pay their debts when there is no written record of them, they clamour for written proof, and reject as worthless the unwritten tradition of the Fathers. But we will not slacken in our defence of the truth. We will not cowardly abandon the cause. The Lord has delivered to us as a necessary and saving doctrine that the Holy Spirit is to be ranked with the Father. Our opponents

Notice, for Basil this is not a matter of secondary importance. This is an attack on the very foundation of our faith, the nature of God, his activity in salvation, his eternal glory, and the way in which we are to relate to him.

This is a "necessary and saving doctrine." Why? Because it is about the very nature of the God we worship.

think differently, and see fit to divide and tear away the Spirit from the Father, and relegate him to the nature of a ministering spirit. Is it not then indisputable that they make their own blasphemy more authoritative than the law of the Lord?...

STAGE 2: THE SPIRIT'S INSEPARABILITY FROM THE WORK OF THE FATHER AND THE SON. [FROM CH'S 16-17]

Let us then return to the point raised from the outset, that in all things the Holy Spirit is inseparable and wholly incapable of being parted from the Father and the Son.

Here we meet the theological idea of "inseparable operations." Because God is one, and therefore inseparable in his eternal relations, he remains one, and united in his temporal actions, even as the three persons of the Trinity act distinctly. Augustine will later state that, "Father, Son and Holy Spirit in the inseparable equality of one substance present a divine unity; and therefore there are not three gods but one God." (De Trinitate 1.7.1) This leads him to say that even though the actions of the Father, Son and Holy Spirit are distinct (the Father addresses the Son from heaven, the Son is born of the virgin Mary, and the Spirit comes down on the day of Pentecost after the Lord's ascension), "just as Father and Son and Holy Spirit are inseparable, so do they work inseparably." (De Trinitae 1.7.2) Inseparable operation defends the Trinity against both modalism (because there really are three persons), and polytheism (because there really is only one God, with one divine mission).

For Basil to introduce the idea here reinforces his point that the Spirit is doing the work of God alone. Like Augustine he draws a line between inseparable operation and inseparable equality. If the Spirit is united with the Father and the Son in his temporal actions, he is inseparable from them in his eternal relation, and divine substance.

St. Paul, in the passage about the gift of tongues, writes to the Corinthians:

> If an unbeliever or an inquirer comes in while everyone is prophesying, they are convicted of sin and are brought under judgment by all, as the secrets of their hearts are laid bare. So they will fall down and worship God, exclaiming, "God is really among you!" (1 Cor 14:24-25).

If then God is known to be present among the prophets because their prophesying is according to the distribution of the gifts of the Spirit, let our adversaries consider what kind of place they will attribute to the Holy Spirit. Let them say whether it is more proper to rank him with God or to thrust him forth to the place of the creature.

Basil begins to assert that 'the Spirit is what the Spirit does.' As we begin to understand rightly his role in salvation, we will see he does God's work. Basil forces us to choose: either the Spirit is God or a creature. There is no middle ground.

In the same way, Peter's words to Sapphira, "How could you conspire to test the Spirit of the Lord? You have not lied just to human beings but to God," show that sins against the Holy Spirit and against God are the same; and thus you might learn that in every operation the Spirit is closely conjoined with, and inseparable from, the Father and the Son.

Acts 5:9 and 5:4

The Father works in various ways, and the Lord serves in various capacities, but all the while the Holy Spirit is present too of his own will, dispensing distribution of the gifts according to each recipient's worth. For, it is said, "There are different kinds of gifts, but the same Spirit distributes them. There are different kinds of service, but the same Lord. There are different kinds of working, but in all of them and in everyone it is the same God at work" (1 Cor 12:4-6). "But all these," it is said, "are the work of one and the same Spirit, and he distributes them to each one, just as he determines" (1 Cor 12:11)...

But when we speak of the plan of salvation for men, made by our great God and Saviour Jesus Christ, who will deny that it has been accomplished through the grace of the Spirit?... In the first place the Lord was anointed by the Spirit, and the Spirit was inseparably present with the very flesh of the Lord, as it is written, "The man on whom you see the Spirit come down and remain is the one who" is "my beloved Son;" and "Jesus of Nazareth" whom "God anointed... with the Holy Spirit." After this every operation was wrought with the co-operation of the Spirit. He was present when the Lord was being tempted by the devil; for, it is said, "Jesus was led by the Spirit into the wilderness to be tempted." He was inseparably with him while working his wonderful works; for, it is said, "it is by the Spirit of God that I drive out demons."

Acts 10:38

Matt 4:1

Matt 12:28

And he did not leave him when he had risen from the dead; for when he renewed man, by breathing on the face of the disciples, and thereby restoring the grace which Adam had lost, (which also came of the inbreathing of God), what did the Lord say? "And with that he breathed on them and said 'Receive the Holy Spirit. If you forgive anyone's sins, their sins are forgiven; if you do not forgive them, they are not forgiven.'"

John 20:22-23. Basil spells out the ways that the Spirit is working inseparably with the Father and the Son in the life, death and resurrection of Jesus, before then outlining the way his ministry continues in the age of the church.

And is it not plain and incontestable that the ordering of the Church is effected through the Spirit? For he gave, it is said, "in the church first of all apostles, second prophets, third teachers, then miracles, then gifts of healing, of helping, of guidance, and of different kinds of tongues." This order

1 Cor 12:28

is established in accordance with the distribution of the Spirit's gifts...

Do you maintain that the Son is numbered under the Father, and the Spirit under the Son, or do you limit your sub-numeration to the Spirit alone?

If, on the other hand, you apply this sub-numeration also to the Son, you revive what is the same impious doctrine, the unlikeness of their essence, the lowliness of rank, the coming into being in later time, and once for all, by this one term, you will plainly again set circling all the blasphemies against the Only-begotten. To controvert these blasphemies would be a longer task than my present purpose admits of; and I am the less bound to undertake it because the impiety has been refuted elsewhere to the best of my ability.

If, on the other hand, they suppose the sub-numeration to benefit the Spirit alone, they must be taught that the Spirit is spoken of together with the Lord in precisely the same manner in which the Son is spoken of with the Father. "The name of the Father and of the Son and of the Holy Spirit" is delivered in like manner, and, according to the co-ordination of words delivered in baptism, the relation of the Spirit to the Son is the same as that of the Son to the Father. And if the Spirit is co-ordinate with the Son, and the Son with the Father, it is obvious that the Spirit is also co-ordinate with the Father.

When then the names are ranked in one and the same co-ordinate series, what room is there for speaking on the one hand of connumeration, and on the other of sub-numeration? No, without exception, what thing ever lost its own nature by being numbered?

Here we meet another argument of Basil's opponents: they take the three persons and assume that number implies a rank, placing the Spirit third, below the Father and the Son. Basil deliberately relates this argument to the earlier Arian controversy around the divinity of Jesus that was so capably refuted by Athanasius. So Basil wants to know: would they extend their argument to the Son and count him below the Father as well?

Matt 28:19

Basil returns to the baptismal formula as a key argument for the Spirit's inseparable operation with the Father and the Son in salvation.

Basil is clear that we are given Father, Son, and Spirit as names to be used, and that it makes sense to count them and get to three. What concerns him is that his opponents have stopped counting and started ranking the person of the Trinity, putting the Spirit at the bottom of the pile.

STAGE 3: THE SPIRIT DESERVES EQUAL HONOUR. [FROM CH'S 19, 22-23]

Basil arrives at his conclusion. It is not enough for him to defend the equal nature of the Spirit; he must defend his equal honour. Right doctrine must come to expression in right worship.

"Even if this is true," they answer, "glory is by no means so absolutely due to the Spirit as to require his exaltation by us in doxologies." But from where do we get evidence of the dignity of the Spirit, "passing all understanding," if not from his communion with the Father and the Son. But our opponents will not recognise this as adequate testimony. To a certain extent though, it is possible for us to understand something of the greatness of his nature and of his unapproachable power, by looking at the meaning of his title, and at the greatness of his works, and his good gifts bestowed on us or rather on all creation. He is called Spirit, as "God is spirit," and "the Lord's anointed, our very life breath." He is called holy, as the Father is holy, and the Son is holy. For creatures, holiness comes from outside, but for the Spirit holiness fills his nature, and it is for this reason that he is described not as sanctified, but as sanctifying. He is called good, as the Father is good, and he who was begotten of the Good is good... He is called upright, as "the Lord is upright," in that he is himself truth, and is himself righteousness, not leaning to one side or to the other, on account of the immutability of his nature. He is called Paraclete, like the Only-begotten, as he himself says, "I will ask the Father, and he will give you another advocate." The Spirit bears these names in common with the Father and the Son, and he gets these titles from his natural and close relationship. From what other source could they be derived? Again he is called royal, the Spirit of truth, and Spirit of wisdom. It is written that "the Spirit of God has made me," and God filled Bezaleel "with the Spirit of God, with wisdom, with understanding, and with knowledge." Such names as these are great and mighty, but they do not exhaust his glory.

John 4:24, Lam 4:20

c.f. Ps 92:15

John 14:16. Paraclete comes from the Greek word used to describe Jesus and the Holy Spirit in John's Gospel. It often has a legal sense of one who advocates for another or gives testimony.

Job 33:4

Exod 31:3

So let's ask, what does the Spirit do? His works are inexpressible in majesty, and innumerable. How shall we form any idea of what extends beyond the ages? How shall we form a conception of what extends beyond the ages? What were his works before creation? How great was the grace which he showered on creation? What power will be exercised by him over the ages to come? He

Ps 32:6 (Basil is following the Greek translation of the Old Testament here, which reads "the heavens were made by the Spirit of his mouth.")

existed; he pre-existed; he co-existed with the Father and the Son before the ages. It follows that, even if you can conceive of anything beyond the ages, you will find the Spirit yet further above and beyond. And if you think of the creation, the powers of the heavens were firmly established by the Spirit. For it is from the Spirit that the heavenly powers derive their close relationship to God, their inability to change to evil, and their continuance in blessedness.

Christ comes, and the Spirit is his forerunner. Christ is incarnate and the Spirit is inseparable. He works miracles, and gifts of healing are through the Holy Spirit. Demons were driven out by the Spirit of God. The devil was brought to naught by the presence of the Spirit. Forgiveness of sins was by the gift of the Spirit, for "you were washed, you were sanctified... in the name of the Lord Jesus Christ and by the Spirit of our God." Through the Spirit we have a close relationship with God, for "God sent the Spirit of his Son into our hearts, the Spirit who calls out, 'Abba, Father.'"

1 Cor 6:11

Gal 4:6

...With these thoughts before us are we to be afraid of going beyond the bounds in the extravagance of the honour we pay? Shall we not rather fear lest, even though we seem to give him the highest names which the thoughts of man can conceive or man's tongue utter, we let our thoughts about Him fall too low?...

Basil delivers a real body slam here. His opponents are asking whether it's ever appropriate to give honour to the Spirit. Basil has flipped the argument over and asks if it is ever possible to give too much honour to the Spirit!

Moreover we can learn about the surpassing excellence of the nature of the Spirit not because he shares the same title as the Father and the Son, and shares in their operations, but also from his being, like the Father and the Son, unapproachable in thought...

Basil reaches the inescapable conclusion. The Spirit is worthy of equal honour with the Father and the Son.

Shall we not then highly exalt him who is in his nature divine, in his greatness infinite, in his operations powerful, in the blessings he confers, good? Shall we not give him glory? And I understand glorifying to mean nothing else than the counting out of the wonders which are his own. It follows then that either we are forbidden by our antagonists even to mention the good things which flow to us from him. Or on the other hand that the mere recapitulation of his attributes is the fullest possible attribution of glory. For not even in the case of the God and Father of our Lord Jesus Christ and of the Only-begotten Son, are we capable of giving them glory otherwise than by recounting, to the extent of our powers, all the wonders that belong to them.

Here Basil helps us to see what honouring the Spirit rightly looks like in practice. We are to recount the glorious wonders of the persons of the Trinity back to them. This is what brings them glory as distinct members of the triune Godhead.

- - - - - - - - EXTRACT ENDS - - - - - - - -

"WHEN WE SEE CHRIST, THE BRIGHTNESS OF GOD'S GLORY, IT IS ALWAYS THROUGH THE ILLUMINATION OF THE SPIRIT."

BASIL
THE GREET
ON THE HOLY SPIRIT, 26.64

★ CONCLUSION ★

For Basil, because the Spirit shares the titles of God and the actions of God, he must also share the essence of God. Action demonstrates essence. If the Spirit does God's work, the Spirit is God, and must be honoured as God. It is on the basis of action and essence that honour is asserted. As a result, the two doxologies stand together: we bring glory to the Father, through the Son, in the Spirit, and yet the Spirit is also to be worshipped and glorified together with the Father and the Son.

And how do we bring him glory? By recounting his glorious wonders back to him. We honour the Spirit rightly as we worship him for his distinct activity in the one divine mission. As John Owen will later re-iterate, "the Holy Spirit is an eternally existing divine substance, the author of divine operations, *and* the object of divine religious worship."

John Owen, *Communion with God* (vol. 2 of The Works of John Owen; London: Banner of Truth, 1965), 400, emphasis added.

Returning to our opening scenario, perhaps it would help Susan and her pastor to distinguish between our access in worship, and the object of our worship. Our access in worship takes into consideration the distinct ministry of the Spirit in the divine mission. The Spirit is self-effacing, with a floodlight ministry on the Son. However, the object of our worship is all three persons in their equal divinity. Just as the Spirit can be distinctly resisted, blasphemed against, quenched, grieved and lied to, so he can be distinctly honoured because of who he is and what he has done.

The question for us, as 21st century evangelicals is, are we guilty of neglecting Basil's second doxology? Is the Holy Spirit in danger of being either assumed or forgotten? We may not deny his presence, activity, or divine status. But in our worship is he treated as a different, *lesser* person than the Father and the Son? Is it even possible that in practical terms we teeter on the edge of the precipice of polytheism?

We counter this as we retell his inexhaustible wonders back to him. How often do you honour the Spirit for his role in saving you? And, for those of us involved in some kind of word ministry, here is one place we could begin.

Why not, as you prepare to minister this week, consider carefully the distinct ways the Spirit has worked, and is working, through the word, to shine his light on Christ. This is one rich vein of the Spirit's economic activity for which he is worthy of honour. Consider his authorship of the Scriptures, and his preservation of the texts. Consider the Spirit's illumination as we read and understand them. Acknowledge and thank him for giving you spiritual life. Reflect on the gifting of the Spirit in raising you up to minister the word, the empowering of the Spirit as you proclaim the Scriptures. Acknowledge further, the life-giving and illuminating work of the Spirit in the hearer. Finally, pause to consider his ongoing ministry in the perseverance and preservation of all the saints. As you reflect on your total dependence on the distinct mission of the Spirit in the ministry he has called you to, bring him glory, together with the Father and the Son.

Questions for further thought and discussion

1. In the Nicene Creed Christians confess their faith in the Holy Spirit,

    the Lord,
    the giver of life,
    who proceeds from the Father and the Son.
    With the Father and the Son he is worshiped and glorified.
    He has spoken through the Prophets.

    How would you now explain the significance of each of those lines?

2. Do you think it would be fair to say the Holy Spirit is assumed or neglected in your church? How could you and your church better "retell his inexhaustible wonders" back to him in private and corporate worship?

TURNING

The Trinity

UP

in the

THE

Old Testament

LIGHTS

For centuries, Christians have confessed their faith through the words of the Nicene Creed:

> *We believe in one God, the Father, the Almighty, maker of heaven and earth...*
> *We believe in one Lord, Jesus Christ, the only Son of God, eternally begotten of the Father...*
> *We believe in the Holy Spirit, the Lord, the giver of life, who proceeds from the Father and the Son...*

CHRIS ANSBERRY serves as Lecturer in Old Testament and Biblical Hebrew as well as Director of Postgraduate Studies at Oak Hill College. He is married to Carolyn and they have four children. Chris and Carolyn are members of Enfield Town Community Church.

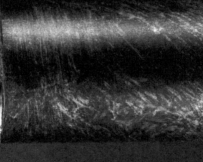

This declaration of one God in three persons distinguishes the Christian faith from other faiths. It is shared by all Christians. But a debated question concerns the Old Testament's contribution to this fundamental Christian belief. Does the Old Testament teach us to confess our faith in this way?

To put the matter bluntly, is the doctrine of the Trinity in the Old Testament? Most respond in the negative. At best, the Old Testament contains signs and shadows that prepare us for the clear revelation of the triune God through the missions of the Son and the Holy Spirit in the "last days" (Acts 2:17; Heb 1:2). Others, by contrast, respond to the question in the affirmative. For those with eyes to see and ears to hear, the triunity of our one God is clear within the pages of the Old Testament.

For helpful discussions of these and other Old Testament traces of the Trinity, see Herman Bavinck, *Reformed Dogmatics* (ed. John Bolt; trans. John Vriend; 4 vols.; Grand Rapids: Baker Academic, 2004) 2:261-64; Geerhardus Vos, *Reformed Dogmatics* (ed. and trans. Richard B. Gaffin, Jr.; 5 vols.; Bellingham: Lexham Press, 2012-2014), 1:38-41; John M. Frame, *The Doctrine of God* (Phillipsburg: P&R, 2002), 631-38.

Both can't be right. So how should we negotiate these divergent responses? The traditional approach has been to wheel out particular Old Testament texts, apply the full range of exegetical tools, and build a particular case. Among other things, this case would rest on the interpretation of at least five features within the Old Testament's witness:

1) The plural form of certain divine names, such as Elohim and Holy One (Prov 9:10; 30:3). Do these forms indicate plurality in the Godhead or should they be understood as "plurals of majesty," intensive forms that express God's inexhaustible fullness?

2) The significance of different divine names, such as Elohim and Yhwh. Do these distinctive names refer to different persons in the Godhead or are they alternative designations for the self-same God?

3) Passages in which God seems to speak as if he is talking amongst himself, such as Gen 1:26 and Isa 6:8. Do these passages reveal inter-Trinitarian conversations? Similar to the plural form of certain divine names, should they be understood as "plurals of majesty?" Or do they depict God in his divine counsel, conversing with other angelic beings?

4) Personified figures who share the attributes of God, such as the Word and Wisdom (Pss 33:6; 56:4, 10; Isa 55:11; Prov 8:1–36). Do these figures represent particular persons of the Trinity or do they simply emphasise certain attributes of God through personification?

5) Those texts that blur the boundary between the angel of the Lord and God (Gen 16:6–13; 22:11–12; 32:30; Hos 12:4; Josh 5:14). In these instances, is the angel of the Lord the pre-incarnate Son? Is the angel of the Lord a created agent through whom all three members of the Trinity inseparably manifest themselves? Or is the angel of the Lord simply an angelic messenger who represents and speaks on behalf of the Lord?

These features fund the traditional approach to the question of the Trinity in the Old Testament. This traditional line of argumentation may be fruitful.

But, in my view, it's not the best way forward, because it tends to end in an exegetical stalemate: one side sees more in the details of these texts; the other sees less. This is not necessarily due to faulty exegesis; rather it's the product of our theological and methodological commitments. These commitments, whether or not they are acknowledged, shape our interpretation of these Old Testament "Trinitarian texts." And when they are brought out into the open, we can understand what all the fuss is about, why certain texts are read in certain ways, and, ultimately, what's at stake with the Trinity and the Old Testament.

The theological and methodological commitments that fund Trinitarian and Christocentric readings of the Old Testament manifest themselves through a variety of approaches. These approaches share a common conclusion regarding the Trinity in the Old Testament; and they share certain theological and methodological commitments. While a typology of approaches may emphasise their similarities at the expense of the variety within each approach, this form of classification allows one to recognise and compare them. That is the goal here. I will summarise the three most common approaches to the Trinity in the Old Testament. For each approach, I will identify a few commitments that shape its understanding of the Trinity in the Old Testament. Following the summary of these approaches, I will return to these commitments, providing a fuller account of them. And I will conclude with some suggestions for how to read the Old Testament with certain theological and methodological commitments. First, the approaches: (1) a history-oriented "no;" (2) a canon-oriented "no...but;" and (3) a Christocentric "yes." Let's take a brief look at each.

THREE ANSWERS

1. THE TRINITY IN THE OT? A HISTORY-ORIENTED "NO"

The first approach privileges history: the historical context of the Old Testament's witness, the historical situations to which it was addressed, the historical audiences who received the text, and the original intention of the human authors, with or without regard to divine authorship. This historical form of reading responds to the question of the Trinity in the Old Testament with a definitive "no." But not all forms of historical reading are the same.

➡ The historical-critical and history-of-religions approaches, for example, view history without reference to God. In the light of this, it's not surprising that the Trinity is not in the Old Testament, for history is often read as an evolution from animism (the worship of created things), to polytheism (the worship of many gods), to henotheism (the worship of one high god among many), to monotheism (the worship of only one God, by the end of the Old Testament), to the doctrine of the Trinity (the worship of one God in three persons, emerging in the early church).

Both of these movements emerged in late 19th century German scholarship. The historical-critical movement sought to examine the OT purely as a historical record of religion, peeling away layers of development in texts and ideas. The history of religions movement was similar; it treated Judaism as one religion amongst many and sought to explain many of its features as dependent on other ancient religions.

■ The grammatical-historical approach, by contrast, demands that history and historical matters be understood from a theological frame of reference. This form of historical reading attends to the original context of the Old Testament text, the final form of the text, and the human author's original intention. For the grammatical-historical approach, historical development is not understood in terms of evolutionary naturalism; rather historical development is understood in terms of God's generous, yet progressive self-revelation. A clear doctrine of the Trinity in the Old Testament, on this account, awaits further disclosure.

While differences remain between these history-oriented approaches, history, however conceived, drives this reading of the Old Testament. And, as we'll discuss below, a particular view of human authorial intention and divine authorial intention as well as an Enlightenment conception of monotheism play a formative role in this historically-driven "no" to the Trinity in the Old Testament.

2. THE TRINITY IN THE OT? A CANON-ORIENTED "NO, BUT…"

The second approach is like the first, in that it is concerned with historical questions. But it refuses to live within the witness of the Old Testament alone. This approach pitches its tent across the witness of the two-Testament canon. The canon of Scripture furnishes a broader context within which to consider the question of the Trinity in the Old Testament; and this context responds to the question with qualified "no… but." By virtue of its concern with the historical particularity of the Old Testament's witness, the canonical approach allows the Old Testament to speak for itself. It seeks to hear the voice of the text on its own terms. This initial hearing reveals that the Old Testament bears unashamed witness to some plurality in the life of the one God. And this unashamed witness to some plurality within the Godhead helps us to reconceptualise the Old Testament's understanding of monotheism. It allows us to recognise that monotheism is not unitarianism; rather it is a term that conveys God's absolute unity, uniqueness, incomparability, and superiority, all of which ought to evoke exclusive loyalty from God's creatures. The canonical approach accounts for the hints of divine plurality in the Old Testament. But the plurality of the one God's life within the Old Testament remains a far cry from an explicit revelation of the number or names of the persons of the triune God. Along with the history-oriented approach, then, the canonical approach acknowledges that the Trinity is not in the Old Testament.

Unitarianism believes God is one person, not three.

This conclusion, however, represents only half of the story, or, perhaps better, half of the canon. The "no" is accompanied by a "but." The relationship between this "no" and "but" is captured by Christopher Seitz, who contends:

> Christian theology does not proceed on the basis of the Old Testament 'evolving' into the New, or the New 'superceding' the Old, but on the basis of a reflection on God's character as revealed in both, each in its own particular idiom.

Christopher R. Seitz, *Word Without End: The Old Testament as Abiding Theological Witness* (Waco: Baylor University Press, 2004), 260.

According to Seitz, the Testaments operate under different "idioms" or ways of speaking about God. The Old Testament privileges God's gracious self-revelation of his name as Yhwh. The New Testament invites God's people to address their one Lord as Father, Son, and Holy Spirit. The language differs; but the God to whom this language refers does not. "God himself," concludes Kavin Rowe, is "the self-same reality to which both Testaments bear witness." The same God is the reality and referent to which both testaments attest, hence the "but" of the canonical approach. The different ways of speaking about God in the two Testaments, however, explain the "no" of the canonical approach: the name of the one God as Father, Son, and Holy Spirit is not yet fully revealed within the pages of the Old Testament.

C. Kavin Rowe, "Biblical Pressure and Trinitarian Hermeneutics," *Pro Ecclesia* 11 (2002): 310.

In addition to the two-Testament witness to the same God through different idioms, the canonical approach offers a second way of considering the Trinity *and* the Old Testament: the practice of retrospective rereading. This practice is modelled by Jesus in Luke 24. And this reading practice takes different forms. Perhaps the best known is the practice of *typological* or *figural* reading. These forms of reading spot connections between people or events within salvation history retrospectively. That is, connections are recognised only after a second or subsequent person or event within the providential unfolding of salvation history. And this retrospective recognition encourages a rereading of the original person or event through the lens of the second. The second person or event supplies fresh insights that enable us to see things actually present in the original account and to produce a fuller reading of the original account.

Typology derives from the Greek word *typos*; the Latin equivalent of *typos* was *figura*, hence figural interpretation. Both typological and figural interpretation refer to readings that explore meaning through the correspondences between two or more texts. For some, typological and figural interpretation are the same. For others, they are not, because figural interpretation is considered a form of allegory. In an attempt to distinguish typology from allegory, many in the post-Reformation era restricted typology to historical people and events. As a result, typology focused on historical patterns. For a helpful discussion of these matters, see Francis M. Young, *Biblical Exegesis and the Formation of Christian Culture* (repr. Peabody: Hendrickson, 2002), 152-57, 189-201.

John 1:1–5, for example, encourages a rereading of Genesis 1. This rereading preserves the meaningfulness and intelligibility of Genesis 1 in its original context. But in the light of John's account of the pre-existence of the Word and the role of the Word in the creative activity of the triune God, one may reread Genesis 1 from this fresh, fuller perspective. This perspective allows us to see that God creates by his Word, a Word that proceeds from him, a Word that is somehow distinct from him, the Word whom we call the second person of the Trinity.

Together with typological or figural readings, the New Testament offers another resource for a retrospective rereading of the Old Testament. When one encounters an Old Testament text where the speakers or actors are ambiguous, the New Testament invites us to identify these ambiguous figures. Perhaps the best example of this form of rereading is Jesus' Trinitarian interpretation of Psalm 110:1. Attributing David's words to the Holy Spirit (Matt 22:43; Mark 12:36), Jesus alerts his audience to the ambiguous identity of the addressee, "my Lord," and asks them to assign an appropriate persona. Who is this person David calls "my Lord?" Identifying ambiguous speakers or actors within the Old Testament through the total witness of Scripture provides the canonical approach with another methodological means to reread the Old Testament retrospectively in the light of the coming of the Son and the Spirit.

For more on this approach, see Fred Sanders, *The Triune God* (New Studies in Dogmatics; Grand Rapids: Zondervan, 2016), 226-31.

While these forms of canonical reading are making a comeback, they may cause the more historically-oriented reader to cringe, because these methods threaten to undermine the progressive nature of revelation or the original context of the Old Testament text. These commitments are to be commended. But it's imperative to recognise that the forms of retrospective rereading discussed above neither negate nor ignore the literal sense of the Old Testament text; rather they create an intertextual and canonical conversation within which actual, but latent meanings may be discovered in the Old Testament text. Retrospective rereading is not a "reading into" the Old Testament something foreign; it is a practice that sees something actually present within the text that may be discerned through the total witness of Scripture and in the light of the coming of the Son and the Holy Spirit.

"The Old Testament may be likened to a chamber richly furnished but dimly lighted; the introduction of light brings into it nothing which was not in it before; but it brings out into clearer view much of what is in it but was only dimly or even not at all perceived before.

The mystery of the Trinity is not revealed in the Old Testament; but the mystery of the Trinity underlies the Old Testament revelation, and here and there almost comes into view.

Thus the Old Testament revelation of God is not corrected by the fuller revelation that follows it, but only perfected, extended and enlarged."

Benjamin B. Warfield, "The Biblical Doctrine of the Trinity," in *Biblical Doctrines*, The Works of Benjamin B. Warfield, vol. 2 (New York: Oxford University Press, 1929), 141-42.

The total witness of Scripture not only funds the canonical approach's "no… but" response to the question of the Trinity in the Old Testament; it also reframes the question as a matter of the Trinity *and* the Old Testament. Fred Sanders describes the task of Trinitarian theology as a "canonical rereading of the identity of God, comprehending the total meaning of the text without effacing or replacing the linear meaning." Attending to both "the total meaning of the text" and its linear or literal-historical meaning may prove difficult. But, as we'll discuss below, it appears the difficulty has to do with our conception of the dual authorship of Scripture. How do we relate the human authorship of Scripture with its divine authorship? And how does this relationship shape our understanding of textual meaning?

Fred Sanders, *The Triune God*, 218.

3. THE TRINITY IN THE OT? A CHRISTOCENTRIC "YES"

The third and final approach is distinctive, for it responds to the question of the Trinity in the Old Testament with a resounding "yes." It's a Christocentric approach. Any approach that operates under the name Christocentric is appealing. After all, who doesn't want to put Jesus at the centre? But the Christocentric approach discussed here remains a particular type of Christocentric approach. It is not the approach of Graeme Goldsworthy or Sidney Greidanus (both of whom would say that Jesus is central to our reading of the OT, but would emphasise progressive revelation and typological readings); rather it is the approach associated in the UK with the theologian Paul Blackham and popularised by evangelist Glen Scrivener, amongst others.

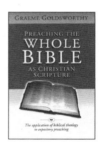 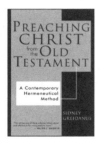

Graeme Goldsworthy, *Preaching the Whole Bible as Christian Scripture* (Nottingham: IVP, 2000).

Sidney Greidanus, *Preaching Christ from the Old Testament* (Grand Rapids, Mich: Eerdmans, 1999).

This approach is harder to evaluate because there are fewer published works arguing for it. But it remains a popular answer to the question of the Trinity in the Old Testament and so deserves attention here. As far as possible, I'll refer to published material by its advocates.

Similar to the canonical approach, the Christocentric approach considers Jesus' encounter with the men on the road to Emmaus and his appearance to his disciples in Luke 24 as the hermeneutical lens through which to read the Old Testament. This lens, however, is focused differently in each approach. Whereas the canonical approach sees Jesus modelling a retrospective reading of the Old Testament in the light of his death and resurrection, the Christocentric approach sees Jesus demonstrating that "the gospel can certainly be understood in the Old Testament just as in the New Testament." The sendings of the Son and the Spirit, it seems, do not reveal anything that is dramatically new, for "the whole gospel of Jesus Christ is set out from the very first page of the Bible."

Paul Blackham, "Appendix 1: Frequently Asked Questions," in Steve Levy, *Bible Overview* (Fearn: Christian Focus, 2008), 304.

Paul Blackham, "Evangelicals and the Bible," in *Not Evangelical Enough! The Gospel at the Centre* (ed. Iain Taylor; Carlisle: Paternoster Press, 2003), 1.

In addition to the accounts in Luke 24, John 1:18 guides the interpretive moves of the Christocentric approach. According to John, "no one has ever seen God, but the one and only Son;" he has made the Father known. If the one and only Son is the only one who has seen God and the only one who reveals the Father, then any Old Testament text that bears witness to the visibility of God, by implication, testifies to the mediatorial activity of the pre-incarnate Son. The second person of the Trinity, from this perspective, mediates God's visible presence in the Old Testament under many names: "God," "the LORD," "the angel of the LORD," "the glory of the LORD" (Exod 16:10), "the Presence (or the Face) of the LORD" (Exod 33:14), the "One traveling in the pillar of cloud and fire," the "Commander of the Lord's army" (Josh 5:14), "Counsellor" (Isa 9:6), "the Lord's servant" (Isa 52:13), and "The Seed" (Gen 3:15), just to name a few.

See Blackham, "Appendix 1: Frequently Asked Questions," 297; Glen Scrivener, *Reading Between the Lines: Old Testament Daily Readings* (Leyland: 10Publishing, 2018), 1:150.

Following the logic of the Christocentric approach, these varied and various appearances of the Son, especially in the book of Exodus, "naturally lead to the confession that one of the divine Persons can be seen and one of the divine Persons cannot be seen." Trinitarian distinctions, on this account, are relatively clear in the Old Testament. Taking encouragement from the early church father Justin Martyr, Blackham contends that the Old Testament itself reveals that "the One God of Israel is not a single person, but a transcendent, invisible Father, an appearing, sent LORD, and the Spirit of the LORD."

Paul Blackham, "The Trinity in the Hebrew Scriptures," in *Trinitarian Soundings in Systematic Theology* (ed. Paul Louis Metzger; London: T&T Clark, 2005), 40.

Blackham, "The Trinity in the Hebrew Scriptures," 42.

Both Luke 24 and John 1:18 provide the Christocentric approach with interpretive principles that, while mentioned in New Testament texts, are considered self-evident and revealed within the Old Testament itself. *Re*reading is unnecessary; all you have to do is read the Old Testament on its own terms. This approach to the Trinity in the Old Testament is driven by two fundamental commitments.

The first is a suspicion of monotheism. The Christocentric approach produces a portrait of a multi-personal God, who differs from the gods worshipped by Jews and Muslims. The second, as we just saw, is a conviction that the Son is the mediator and the visible image of the invisible God. If God is ever seen, it is the Son who is seen.

Blackham, "Evangelicals and the Bible," 100.

These two commitments shape the Christocentric approach's reading of the Old Testament. It is a reading that identifies the different persons of the Trinity in the Old Testament. And it is a reading that has little room for progressive revelation. This is not surprising, since the content of God's self-revelation of himself and the gospel is "set out from the very first page of the Bible." Revelation is not progressive. In fact, progression is the wrong word. Revelation, according to the Christocentric approach, is perspectival. The Old Testament looks forward to what is revealed; the New Testament looks back on that same revelation. These methodological commitments open new horizons for speaking about the Trinity in the Old Testament. But they also raise significant questions concerning the doctrine of God and the nature of revelation.

THREE KEY ISSUES

Taken together, these three approaches offer different responses to the question of the Trinity in the Old Testament. The responses differ because they are underwritten by different theological and methodological commitments. These commitments were mentioned in the discussion above, but they deserve specific comment. Fittingly, there are three: (1) a doctrine of God; (2) the nature of revelation; and (3) the relationship between the human and divine authorship of Scripture.

1. THE DOCTRINE OF GOD

Blackham, "The Trinity in the Hebrew Scriptures," 35.

While each of the approaches we've surveyed are operating with a doctrine of God, the Christocentric approach foregrounds the issue and is at pains to emphasise the Trinitarian nature of God. For Blackham, Christian theology has all too often concealed the Old Testament's "Trinitarian faith." Following the theologians Jürgen Moltmann and Colin Gunton (Blackham's doctoral supervisor), he contends that classical theism (the traditional doctrine of God) starts in the wrong place:

Blackham, "The Trinity in the Hebrew Scriptures," 35-36.

...a classical approach to the doctrine of God... begins with a definition of a single divine essence before later (and usually more briefly) dealing with the three divine persons... If the most important and foundational claims about the Living God can be made before the actual divine Persons are even mentioned, to what extent can such a doctrine of God claim to be genuinely Trinitarian? If the so-called *essence* of God is defined *a priori*, in advance of a careful investigation of the Three Persons who actually *are* the Living God, then we must expect that our thinking about God will tend to default to a kind of monotheism.

That is, defined by appealing to a prior assumption about what essence means.

According to Blackham, classical theism's attention to the substance of the one God not only hinders its account of the three persons and restricts its perception of the Trinity in the Old Testament; it also commits a more heinous crime: it nourishes "the contemporary assumption that Islam, Judaism and Christianity all worship the same God." Classical theism, on this account, produces a frightful form of monotheism. The solution to this "Yahweh-unitarian" conception of God is less attention to the divine essence and more attention to the divine persons.

Blackham, "The Trinity in the Hebrew Scriptures," 36.

This move may allow us to discern the activity of the divine persons in salvation history and to recover aspects of the Old Testament's "Trinitarian faith." But it comes at a cost. By focusing on the divine persons at the expense of the divine substance, it flattens out the intimate and dynamic link between the *economic* Trinity (the actions of the triune persons in the world) and the *immanent* Trinity (God's eternal being) in classical accounts of the doctrine of God and perpetuates the perceived problem by leaving the unity of God's essence open to question. In fact, the lack of attention to the unity of God's essence invites the accusation of subordinationism.

Let me be clear: the Christocentric approach does not claim that the Son is subordinate to the Father; and it does not necessarily lead to the subordination of the Son to the Father. But the approach does raise the question of subordinationism. As noted above, the Christocentric approach claims that "The Most High God" is invisible, while the Son is visible. This suggests that the Father and the Son possess attributes that the other does not; it implies that they do not share the *same* divine substance. By focusing on the Son's visibility in salvation history, this sort of reading carries the potential to introduce a hierarchy or distinction in the eternal being of God. Classical theism not only guards against such distinctions; it also helps us deal with Scripture's dual claim that God is *both* visible and invisible. Following Michael Allen, the classical approach allows us "to speak of the visibility of the invisible God." While God manifested himself visibly at many times and in various ways within the Old Testament, the Son's incarnation and the Spirit's descent at Christ's baptism as well as at

Michael Allen, *Grounded in Heaven: Recentering Christian Hope and Life on God* (Grand Rapids: Eerdmans, 2018), 83.

Pentecost represent distinct, "visible missions," whereby the "Son and the Spirit alike are visibly involved in manifesting God's mission to the world." God is truly visible in certain Old Testament accounts. God is truly and uniquely visible through the coming of the Son and the Spirit. And yet, the triune God also remains invisible, even in the coming of the Son and the Spirit, because God's own vision and the visibility of the divine persons to one another is not the same as our creaturely vision of God. Our creaturely perspective does not match God's perspective.

It is clear that the Christocentric approach is committed to a doctrine of God, just not the classical doctrine of God. This produces a Trinitarian reading that leaves the unity of the Godhead open to question, that invites unhelpful distinctions between the Father and the Son, and that minimises the revelation offered through the coming of the Son and the Spirit.

In addition to the (in)visibility of God, a word on monotheism is in order. Monotheism surfaced in the history-oriented approach, where the progressive revelation of God as the only God ruled out the Trinity in the Old Testament. Monotheism also surfaced in the Christocentric approach, where it was defined as a denial of Trinitarianism, a definition that would lump the Christian God in with the god of the Jews and Muslims. And yet, when we turn to the Old Testament and consider its claims about God, a much different picture emerges. The Old Testament neither denies the existence of other gods nor conceals the complexity or plurality of the one God of Israel. Without the existence of other gods, texts that claim YHWH's supremacy over the gods would make no sense; there would be no comparison (Exod 15:11; 1 Kgs 8:23; Ps 97:9). And without the existence of other gods, texts that claim YHWH has defeated certain gods or that his people have worshipped unknown gods would make no sense (Exod 12:12; Deut 32:17; Ps 82). Monotheism, within the Old Testament, includes God's superiority over other gods as well as his plurality. In a word, monotheism concerns God's uniqueness. As the creator of and sovereign ruler over the cosmos, the God of Israel is "in a class of his own," distinct from "all other reality." And this uniqueness evokes exclusive devotion and worship.

This definition of monotheism is at odds with the working definition of monotheism in the history-

Allen, *Grounded in Heaven*, 78.

On this, see Allen, *Grounded in Heaven*, 84.

See Michael Heiser, *The Unseen Realm: Recovering the Supernatural Worldview of the Bible* (Bellingham: Lexham Press, 2015).

Richard Bauckham, *Jesus and the God of Israel: God Crucified and Other Studies on the New Testament's Christology of Divine Identity* (Milton Keynes: Paternoster, 2008), 86–87.

oriented and Christocentric approaches. In fact, as Nathan MacDonald and Richard Bauckham have helpfully shown, the history-oriented and Christocentric approaches' understanding of monotheism is closer to the definition provided by the Enlightenment. The term *monotheism* is the invention of the Enlightenment; and its definition of the term (emphasising belief in one God and one God only) has been projected onto the Old Testament rather than derived from it. The definitions of monotheism in the history-oriented and Christocentric approaches obscure the Old Testament's witness to the complex and unique divine identity of the God of Israel; and these misguided definitions of monotheism minimise the conceptual space created by the Old Testament for the revelation of the Son and the Spirit in the divine identity of the one God of Israel.

See Bauckham's work just mentioned and MacDonald's *Deuteronomy and the Meaning of "Monotheism"* (Tübingen: Mohr Siebeck, 2003).

2. PROGRESSIVE REVELATION

The missions of the Son and the Spirit play a formative role in our doctrine of God and its implications for the Trinity in the Old Testament. These missions also shape the second theological commitment: our view of revelation. The history-oriented approach and the canonical approach both operate with a view of progressive revelation. This progression is conceived differently by the different approaches. Whereas historical-critical and history-of-religions approaches tend to view *history* in naturalistic and evolutionary terms, grammatical-historical and canonical approaches tend to view *revelation* as progressive. The progressive nature of revelation is not due to the development of human ideas about God; rather it is due to *God's* progressive disclosure of his person and redemptive purposes. Channelling the Dutch theologian Geerhardus Vos, Scott Swain provides two reasons for the progressive nature of God's self-revelation:

Scott R. Swain, *Trinity, Revelation, and Reading: A Theological Introduction to the Bible and its Interpretation* (London: T&T Clark, 2011), 23.

First, the infinite riches of God's triune life and purpose can only be communicated to finite creatures in a finite manner... Second, and more importantly, God's mysterious plan to sum up all things in Christ itself requires a long, historical process in order to be realized... Because God's redemptive economy takes time to unfold, his revelation of that economy takes time to unfold as well."

The organic progression of God's gracious self-revelation contributes to the historically and canonically-oriented approaches' response to the question of the Trinity in the Old Testament. Their respective "no" and "no... but" is rooted in the belief that the mystery of the one God's triune life is not revealed until the fullness of time (Gal 4:4; Eph 1:10), with the coming of the Son and the Spirit in the "last days" (Acts 2:17; Heb 1:2).

Blackham, "Appendix 1: Frequently Asked Questions," 302, emphasis original.

This is not the case, however, with the Christocentric approach. While Blackham responds to the question *"Is the revelation of God 'progressive'?"* with a clear "yes," the progressive nature of revelation is downplayed significantly. As noted above, the Christocentric approach describes revelation as perspectival rather than progressive. The content of revelation does not develop. Instead, the perspective changes: one either looks forward to the sendings of the Son and the Spirit or looks back. The gospel may have "received fresh expressions as the Biblical story unfolded;" but it remained "the same from first to last." The relative lack of progression in the Christocentric account of revelation seems to be due to its disdain for the worst parts of liberal scholarship and its hostility to theological interpretations of history. In one place, Blackham speaks against the attempt "to confine the theological truths of the earlier books to a hypothetical embryonic faith, allowing it to slowly grow as the history of the world develops, *in the manner of the theory of progressive revelation*." In other words, Blackham defines progressive revelation as a natural evolutionary process by which truth emerges in the course of human history. But this is a unique definition, and a straw man. Advocates of progressive revelation, as noted above, have always meant something else.

Both quotes are from Blackham, "Appendix 1: Frequently Asked Questions," 302.

Blackham, "Evangelicals and the Bible," 100, emphasis mine.

3. DIVINE AND HUMAN AUTHORSHIP

The third and final commitment is inextricably linked to our doctrine of God and view of revelation; it concerns the relationship between the human and divine authorship of Scripture. To be specific, it concerns whether the intention or meaning of the human author is identical with that of the divine author.

The relationship between the human and divine authorship of Scripture can be described in (you guessed it) three ways:

➡ The first claims that the human author's intent is equivalent to the divine author's intent. Some from the canonical camp might argue this is the case; most from the history-oriented and the Christocentric approaches would say this is certainly the case.

➡ The second option claims that the human author's intent is consistent with the divine author's meaning, but acknowledges that God would have a more exhaustive understanding of the text's significance.

G. K. Beale, "The Cognitive Peripheral Vision of Biblical Authors," WTJ 76 (2014): 264.

➡ The third option, by contrast, claims that the divine author's intent is fuller than the human author's and not necessarily understood or perceived by the human author. The meaning or intention of the Old Testament author is never negated, but the text becomes the divine author's vehicle for latent "meanings unsuspected by the original authors and readers."

Richard B. Hays, *Reading Backwards: Figural Christology and the Fourfold Gospel Witness* (London: SPCK, 2015), 15.

All this to say, our understanding of the dual authorship of Scripture is not an abstract exercise; it's an understanding that shapes our reading of Scripture in general and our response to the Trinity in the Old Testament in particular.

DRAWING THINGS TOGETHER

Different approaches to the Trinity in the Old Testament operate under different theological and methodological commitments that produce different responses to the revelation of the triune God prior to the coming of the Son and the Spirit. Although there is clearly room for debate amongst evangelicals, I'm convinced the canonical approach is the best. With the history-oriented approach, it respects the historical particularity of the Old Testament text and rightly recognises the progressive nature of revelation; but unlike the history-oriented approach, it adequately accounts for the divine authorship of the whole canon and allows the New Testament to guide our rereading of the Old. With the Christocentric approach, the canonical approach rightly insists that the God of Israel is the eternal triune God; but unlike the Christocentric approach, it refuses to overread the Old Testament. And it respects the Old Testament's manner of speaking about God, who is not clearly revealed as only three persons, let alone by the name Father, Son, and Holy Spirit.

When the Trinity is considered within the total witness of the two-testament canon, we discover that the Old Testament is essential for our understanding of the triunity of the one God. The contributions of the Old Testament, however, are limited neither to prooftexts and personifications nor accounts of complexity and multiplicity in the Godhead. These contributions are also found in the Old Testament's framework and its idiom or manner of speaking about God, which is adopted by the New Testament.

The Old Testament provides the necessary framework for the clear revelation of the triune God. This framework is constructed through the Old Testament's rich description of God's character and actions. Far from depicting an impersonal, unitarian deity, the Old Testament bears witness to the one, unique God of Israel, who creates through wisdom, speaks through his word, enlivens through his Spirit, and reveals himself through intimate, covenant relationship with his people. That is, the Old Testament reveals a unique God who is not Unitarian; it testifies to a God who exists "in a class of his own," who remains distinct from "all other reality," yet graciously relates to his creatures in such a way that allows for "distinction within the unique identity of the one God." This is the Old Testament's exposition of monotheism. And this exposition furnished the necessary framework for the

Christopher Seitz, "The Trinity in the Old Testament," in *The Oxford Handbook of the Trinity* (ed. Gilles Emery and Matthew Levering; Oxford: Oxford University Press, 2011), 30.

Richard Bauckham, *God Crucified: Monotheism and Christology in the New Testament* (Carlisle: Paternoster Press, 1998), 22.

clear revelation of the triune God through the coming of the Son and the Holy Spirit; it created the conditions through which the New Testament writers included Christ and the Spirit in the divine identity of the one God of Israel without compromising or departing from scriptural monotheism.

In the light of this framework, it's not surprising that the New Testament writers included Christ and the Spirit in the unique divine identity of the one God of Israel through the Old Testament's idiom or manner of speaking about God. While the Trinitarian significance of many Old Testament images and expressions could be mentioned, the New Testament's use of the God of Israel's sole personal name, YHWH, captures the Old Testament's contributions to the Trinitarian semantics of the New. With few exceptions, whenever the New Testament quotes Old Testament texts that include the name YHWH, it follows the practice of the Septuagint and renders God's personal name as *kyrios* (LORD). As Richard Bauckham and Kavin Rowe have demonstrated, the use of this name within the New Testament illuminates the Old Testament's relation to Trinitarian doctrine. Reiterating the *Shema* (Deut 6:4-5), Jesus declares that "the LORD is one" (Mark 12:29), which one of the teachers of the law accurately interprets as "and there is no other besides him" (Mark 12:32). According to the total witness of the New Testament, however, this one LORD is three: the Father is LORD of heaven and earth (Matt 11:25); Jesus is LORD, the one to whom every knee will bow and every tongue swear allegiance (Phil 2:9-11; Isa 45:18-23) as well as the name on which everyone must call to be saved (Acts 2:21; Rom 10:13; Joel 2:32); and the Spirit is LORD (2 Cor 3:17). The singular *name* of the one LORD is three: the *name* of the Father, and of the Son, and of the Holy Spirit (Matt 28:19). The Old Testament's rendering of the one God's sole personal name funds the New Testament's Trinitarian idiom; it provides the New Testament writers with the means to uphold both the oneness of God and his name as LORD Father, LORD Son, and LORD Holy Spirit.

These are just a few of the Old Testament's contributions to Trinitarian doctrine. When the Old Testament's manner of speaking about God, its unashamed witness to plurality in the life of the one God, and its conception of God's absolute uniqueness are heard on their own terms, we can begin to understand that the triunity of

See Bauckham, *Jesus and the God of Israel*, 60-95.

See Bauckham, *Jesus and the God of Israel*, 182-232; Rowe, "Biblical Pressure and Trinitarian Hermeneutics," 299-306.

Rowe, "Biblical Pressure and Trinitarian Hermeneutics," 304.

our one God clearly revealed in the witness of the New Testament stands in continuity with the Old. When we submit to the progressive way in which God has chosen to reveal himself, we can see, through the lens of the New Testament and with the light of the Spirit, the signs and shadows of God's triunity in the Old Testament with more clarity. When we follow the direction of Jesus and the apostles and reread the Old Testament in view of the reality of God's triunity, we can perceive things that God has graciously placed in his word all along. And when we privilege God's clear revelation of himself as the Father, who sent his Son and the Spirit of his Son into our hearts at the fullness of time, we are taught to confess our faith in one God, Father, Son and Holy Spirit.

Questions for further thought and discussion

1. Chris identifies three key issues that are involved when we ask about the Trinity in the Old Testament: the doctrine of God, progressive revelation, and the divine and human authorship of Scripture. Can you state clearly why each of those are in the mix? How do definitions of monotheism fit in? And what does the visibility of God have to do with this question?

2. Given Chris' argument here, how are both the Old Testament and the New Testament vital for our doctrine of God? How might it lead to a higher view of Jesus if the Old Testament begins by identifying Israel's God as the supreme "I AM" before Jesus arrives and takes that name onto his lips? (e.g. in John 8:58 and 18:5-6).

HOLY, HOLY, HOLY!

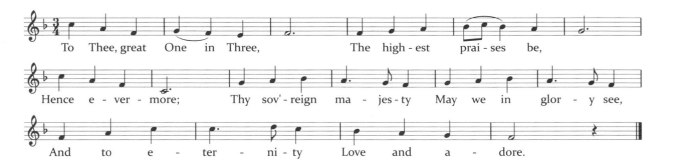

To Thee, great One in Three, The high-est prai-ses be, Hence e-ver-more; Thy sov'-reign ma-jes-ty May we in glor-y see, And to e-ter-ni-ty Love and a-dore.

True worship is Trinitarian. There is no alternative. Either we worship the God who is Father, Son, and Spirit, or we commit idolatry.

MATT MERKER serves as an elder and part of the pastoral staff at Capitol Hill Baptist Church in Washington, D.C. His congregational songs, including *He Will Hold Me Fast*, are available at mattmerkermusic.com. He lives on Capitol Hill with his wife and their two children.

🐦 *@MerkerMatt*

Thankfully, those who are born again know the triune God whether or not they possess precise language to describe his nature. To be a Christian *is* to worship God as Father in union with the Son through the indwelling of the Holy Spirit. As Fred Sanders has put it, evangelicals are "Trinitarian deep down," no matter how vaguely we may understand the intricacies of persons and processions, substance, and relations. There is simply no other God who exists, no other God who saves.

Fred Sanders, *The Deep Things of God: How the Trinity Changes Everything*, 2nd ed. (Wheaton, IL: Crossway, 2017), 14.

When God gathers the church for corporate worship, then, it is the *triune* God who is at work in us – there is no other. Whether Christians consciously recognise it or not, a church meeting is a thoroughly Trinitarian phenomenon.

Yet, pastors shouldn't be content merely to acknowledge that corporate worship resonates with Trinitarian overtones. We should aspire for our congregations to know, hear, obey, commune with, and adore God *as* Trinity each Lord's Day.

Why? Because doxology and theology reinforce each other. *Lex orandi, lex credendi*, the saying goes: "the law of prayer is the law of belief." How we worship God shapes our understanding of him. Since the God who assembles us for his praise is triune, our corporate meetings should help us understand his nature. If we suppress or ignore the doctrine of the Trinity when the church gathers, we risk allowing the latent idolatries of the human heart to flourish. False notions of God spring up in soil deficient in Trinitarian realities.

To put it more positively, corporate worship is discipleship. Just as water carves canyons in the ground one rainfall at a time, church gatherings shape our hearts, week in and week out. Thus, the more self-consciously Trinitarian our services are, the more our church members should understand the Trinity over time. Knowing the triune God more deeply leads to loving him more completely.

My purpose in this article, then, is twofold. First, I aim to demonstrate the Trinitarian dimensions of corporate worship. When God's people meet, there is a theological grammar or logic that undergirds all we do, and this logic is triune, through and through. As a church elder writing for fellow elders, my prayer is that we would become more conscious of these Trinitarian dimensions when we plan and lead services.

Second, I will share concrete suggestions for how pastors can highlight God's triune nature in the standard elements of a worship gathering. Although efforts to increase awareness of the Trinity in corporate worship will undoubtedly take different forms depending on one's theological heritage and liturgical tradition, I trust that offering specific ideas will spark further study, discussion, and application.

THE TRINITARIAN DIMENSIONS OF CORPORATE WORSHIP

For the Christian, all of life is worship (Rom 12:1). But God also calls his people to meet regularly to hear his word, give him thanks, and spur one another on in Christ (Col 3:16, Eph 5:19-20, Heb 10:24-25). This is *corporate* worship, when the local church gathers in Jesus' name as his authorised witnesses on earth (Matt 18:20). We congregate as those who have been baptised "in the name of the Father and of the Son and of the Holy Spirit" (Matt 28:19). Having tasted a salvation that is gloriously Trinitarian (Eph 1:3-14), we gather to enjoy fellowship with the blessed Trinity. It follows that in some sense, when we meet to engage with God, his triune nature informs the content and character of the event.

How? Consider two trajectories or dimensions that coexist when God's people gather. John Witvliet helpfully summarises these "directional movements" as first "God's coming to the church" and second "the church's response to God." Both are deeply Trinitarian.

John D. Witvliet, "The Trinitarian DNA of Christian Worship: Perennial Themes in Recent Literature" in *Colloquium Journal* (New Haven, CT: Yale Institute of Sacred Music), 2005: 3. Available as a PDF online.

THE TRIUNE GOD MINISTERS TO US

First, corporate worship is a gracious act of the triune God for his people. It is all too common to conceive of a church meeting as primarily or exclusively our "service" to God. There is a grain of truth in that expression, but it is secondary in theological order and importance. First and foremost, the God who is Trinity serves his people.

God, as Trinity, knows no lack. The love between Father, Son, and Spirit is infinitely satisfying. Michael Reeves puts it well:

Michael Reeves, *Delighting in the Trinity: An Introduction to the Christian Faith* (Downers Grove, IL: IVP, 2012), 127, emphasis original.

Other gods *need* worship and service and sustenance. But this God needs nothing. He has life in himself – and so much so that he is brimming over. His glory is inestimably good, overflowing, self-giving.

Worship, then, is not fundamentally about what we offer to God, for "what do you have that you did not receive?" (1 Cor 4:7). As we see in Psalm 50, *God* takes the initiative to reveal himself by his word (4:1-3), *God* summons his covenant people to gather (4:5), and *God* does not need our sacrifices, for he owns the universe (4:10-12). Rather, when the church meets, the triune God offers himself to us. He assembles us as the temple of his Holy Spirit, united to his Son, and he speaks, gives, blesses, nourishes, comforts, and pours out his kindness.

In other words, in all our dealings with God, he makes the first move. Theologically speaking, there is no one who "seeks" after God in worship (Ps 14:2). Only one "seeker" attends your church meeting: the triune God. Jesus taught, "The hour is coming, and is now here, when the true worshippers will worship the Father in spirit and truth, for the Father is seeking such people to worship him. God is spirit, and those who worship him must worship in spirit and truth" (John 4:23-24). What a glorious wonder! God "seeks" us. The Father gives us his Son, who is the Truth, and his Spirit, who bears witness about the Son (John 14:6, 15:26). We can therefore say that God generates our worship by his triune self-revelation and gracious redemption. We are worshippers only because the Son has sent us the Spirit of truth from the Father (John 15:26).

Then, having transformed us from idolaters into true worshippers, God also gathers us as his people each Lord's Day and works in our midst. Charles Cranfield argues,

C. E. B. Cranfield, "Divine and Human Action: The Biblical Concept of Worship," *Interpretation* 12 (1958), 389.

...in each particular act of worship the chief actor is not man but God, the divine action consisting in the presence of Jesus Christ in fulfilment of his promise, 'Lo, I am with you always, even unto the end of the world.'

Christ himself is the chief Shepherd, present by his Spirit, who feeds us from the green pastures and quiet waters of his word, that we may know and glorify the Father.

Of course, this doesn't invalidate human responsibility in the worship gathering. God does command us to give him the honour due his name. But amazingly, when we respond to God, the triune God is at work in us, "for it is God who works in you to will and to act in order to fulfill his good purpose." (Phil 2:13). Our worship is "to him," but also "from him" and "through him," to echo Paul's doxology in Romans 11:36.

What impact should the reality of God's initiative in the church's gathering have on how we conceive of corporate worship? Here are two vital takeaways.

First, because the triune God takes the lead in gathering the church, the worship service is an expression of his grace. It is all too easy for our fallen hearts to conceive of Sunday morning as our attempt to gain God's favour, to appease him, to earn his blessing. Trinitarian worship has a wonderful way of dismantling such instincts. Engaging with God is only possible because the Father has made us his people in the Son, whose redemptive work the Holy Spirit applies to the elect. Worship, like salvation, is a gift that is free for us because the Son paid an infinite cost.

Second, God's Trinitarian initiative means that we gather to receive from him. We are weak children whom our Father delights to sustain by granting us nourishment in his Son by his Spirit. We feed on Christ in his word and Supper. Cranfield again observes,

Cranfield, "Divine and Human Action," 392.

The human action in worship is a hearing and a receiving... This hearing of the word of God, hearing what the Lord of the church wants to say to his church in its actual situation, is the primary task of the church, the basic human action in worship.

Is it somehow man-centred to stress that we come to church to receive from God? Not at all, for God glorifies himself by proving faithful to provide for us. It is precisely by admitting our need for the triune God of grace that we glorify his sufficiency.

IN UNION WITH CHRIST, WE RESPOND TO GOD

The second trajectory of corporate worship, from the church upward to God, is as Trinitarian as the first. Our response to God in worship, which exalts him and edifies other believers, is nothing less than communion with the Trinity.

The doctrine of union with Christ is central in this Godward trajectory of corporate worship. How is it that sinners can offer any sort of praise to an infinitely holy God? Because we are one with the Son: "through him we both have access to the Father by one Spirit" (Eph 2:18). John Owen put it this way:

John Owen, *Of Communion with God the Father, Son, and Holy Ghost*, in *The Works of John Owen*, ed. W. H. Goold, vol. 2 (Edinburgh: Banner of Truth Trust, 1965), 8-9, emphasis original.

Our communion, then, with God consists in his *communication of himself to us, with our returning to him* of that which he requires and accepts, flowing from the *union* which in Jesus Christ we have with him.

It is because the Spirit has united us by faith with Christ that we can return to God the praise he requires. We know that the Father accepts our worship because we offer it in and through the beloved Son, with whom he is well pleased.

Christ is our great high priest and mediator. In his active obedience, he lived a life of perfect worship before the Father. In his passive obedience, he gave himself as the unblemished offering of worship *par excellence*. Christ is both priest and sacrifice, the book of Hebrews insists (Heb 8:1, 10:14). As our representative before the Father, he shares our flesh and blood (Heb 2:14). He is the true worship leader who says "I will declare your name to my brothers and sisters; in the assembly I will sing your praises" (Heb 2:12).

This means that we don't come before God on our own. How could we? We worship only in and through Christ. By his Spirit, he dwells in us on earth *and* represents us in heaven. Edmund Clowney says it well:

In the Spirit, we worship in heaven in the great assembly where Jesus is. In the Spirit, Jesus worships on earth in the congregation where we are. In heaven and on earth, we are in the presence of Jesus.

Edmund Clowney, "Corporate Worship: A Means of Grace," in *Give Praise to God: A Vision for Reforming Worship*, ed. Philip Graham Ryken, Derek W. H. Thomas, and J. Ligon Duncan III (Phillipsburg, NJ: P&R, 2003), 96.

In other words, we can only be confident that God hears our praises *because* worship is Trinitarian. We worship through and in Christ, our mediator and high priest, by Spirit-wrought union with him. Moreover, corporate worship is not an attempt to shout loud enough so that a vague, far off deity might hear us. Far from it. When the church gathers, we relate personally and corporately with the triune God of love. We enjoy the "grace of the Lord Jesus Christ and the love of God and the fellowship of the Holy Spirit" (2 Cor 13:14).

Consider a few ways this truth shapes our corporate worship gatherings.

First, our worship should be both "Christ-centred" and Trinitarian. The two aims are not mutually exclusive but complementary. Since we approach the Father in union with the Son, and the Spirit bears witness about the Son, it is appropriate for our services to centre on the person and work of Christ. So argues Bryan Chapell:

Christian worship inevitably makes Christ's work its central theme... Christo-centrality commits us to honour Father, Son, and Holy Spirit by worshipping them in the context of the redeeming work that culminates in Christ.

Bryan Chapell, *Christ-Centered Worship: Letting the Gospel Shape Our Practice* (Grand Rapids: Baker Academic, 2009), 113-114.

We must resist the temptation toward a half-baked Trinitarianism in corporate worship where we may frequently *mention* the Father, Son, and Spirit, but fail to let the whole Trinitarian character of redemption in Christ inform the way that we approach God.

Second, pastors and worship leaders shouldn't focus our attention on generating a particular sort of emotional "experience." I fear, even if it is sub-conscious and implicit, that the unstated goal of much modern evangelical worship is to provide a feeling of inspiration, some sort of encounter with the sublime. Trinitarian worship offers something far better. When the church gathers, we come before the Father in the Son as those who are filled by the Spirit. To be sure, communion with this glorious God will frequently move, amaze, and transform us. But it may just as often involve lament, confession, or desperation, as we see in the Psalms. We should plan our services around the reality that God meets with us in Christ and accepts our praise in him. Trusting his wisdom, we can leave the emotional impact up to him.

Third, a corporate worship gathering is primarily for believers, even while it should still have a powerful evangelistic effect. Corporate worship *is* fellowship with God in Christ by the Spirit. Believers and non-believers, by definition, encounter the service differently. To arrange the form and content of a service primarily with an eye to engaging or "reaching" unbelievers is thus to commit an error of category confusion. Paul again and again insists that the church in Corinth prioritise edifying the body when they meet (1 Cor 14:5, 12, 26). Trinitarian worship does just that. As we use the Spirit's gifts, exalting Christ, we seek "the common good" of the church (1 Cor 12:7). We should, of course, strive for our worship to be intelligible to "an unbeliever or an inquirer" who attends (1 Cor 14:24), but that is just the point: such a person is not (yet!) "in" on the glories of union with the triune God. As we prophesy intelligibly in the Spirit to edify one another, God is pleased to give life to the dead. So, it turns out that aiming at edification through exalting the triune God in corporate worship is in fact the biblical way to be evangelistic when the church gathers.

THE TRINITY IN THE ELEMENTS OF CORPORATE WORSHIP

Let's turn now to the major components of a Sunday service. As we do, imagine a gourmet meal with many dishes prepared by one chef. The various courses all have different flavours and textures, yet each dish reveals the chef's signature style. In a similar way, the different elements of a worship service each contribute to the whole feast, a unified banquet of communion with the God who is Trinity. Each part should exude a rich Trinitarian aroma, even if it is more pronounced in certain sections of the service and subtler in others.

How can pastors highlight, throughout the service, that it is the *triune* God who serves us at his table?

BAPTISM AND THE LORD'S SUPPER

As signs and seals of union with Christ, baptism and the Lord's Supper are two vital means by which the triune God ministers to his people.

In baptism, the local church identifies a believer with the name of the Father, Son, and Holy Spirit (Matt 28:19). The convert who has passed through the waters of baptism is buried with Christ in his death (Rom 6:4).

Here, though in a different order, I will follow the Westminster Confession of Faith (XXV.1) in its conclusion on what acts of worship God has ordained for his gathered people, which some have summarised as "Read the Bible, preach the Bible, pray the Bible, sing the Bible, and see the Bible [in the sacraments of baptism and the Lord's Supper]." See J. Ligon Duncan III, "Foundations for Biblically Directed Worship," in *Give Praise to God*, ed. Ryken, Thomas, and Duncan, 65.

When Jesus identified with his people in baptism, the Father declared that he was well pleased with his Son and sent the Spirit to rest on him (Matt 3:16-17). Now, when we identify with Christ through baptism, we do so with confidence that the Father is well pleased with us who bear the Spirit of Christ.

To accentuate the Trinity at baptism, then, pastors would do well to explain baptism in all its rich new covenant meaning. Baptism isn't mainly a badge of individual discipleship – an inspiring way to get one's Christian life started with a splash, if you'll excuse the pun. It is, rather, both a funeral for the sinner who is buried with Christ, and a marriage vow, as the believer formally pledges his or her identity as part of Christ's covenant bride. I encourage pastors to develop concise yet pithy Trinitarian language for describing what's going on at baptism: "In just a moment, we'll baptise Joe as a sign that he is united to Christ and so is united to us as Christ's body, sharing the same Father and Spirit."

It is equally vital to emphasise union with Christ at the Lord's Table. The Supper is not only an act of remembrance of Christ's sacrifice and anticipation of his glorious kingdom. It is also communion between the church and her Lord: "Is not the cup of thanksgiving for which we give thanks a participation in the blood of Christ? And is not the bread that we break a participation in the body of Christ?" (1 Cor 10:16). The Son is seated at the right hand of the Father to represent and intercede for his people (Heb 10:12). And yet, by the ministry of the Holy Spirit, believers enjoy fellowship with the Son at the Table. So argued Calvin:

The Lord bestows this benefit [of participation] upon us through his Spirit so that we may be made one in body, spirit, and soul with him. The bond of this connection is therefore the Spirit of Christ, with whom we are joined in unity, and is like a channel through which all that Christ himself is and has is conveyed to us.

John Calvin, *Institutes of the Christian Religion*, ed. John T. McNeill, trans. Ford Lewis Battles (Louisville: Westminster John Knox Press, 1960), IV.xvii.12.

See, e.g., Heidelberg Catechism Qu.66 and Westminster Confession of Faith XXVII.1.

As the Reformed confessions teach, this fellowship with Christ by his Spirit at the Table is a gift of God the Father, given to seal his promises to us.

On this point, see J. Todd Billings, *Remembrance, Communion, and Hope: Rediscovering the Gospel at the Lord's Table* (Grand Rapids, MI: Eerdmans, 2018), 16 as well as page 68 onwards.

With that in mind, pastors miss a major opportunity to highlight the Trinity if we neglect to explain the Supper in terms of the Father's gift to enjoy present communion with Christ by his Spirit. In my congregation, we often introduce the Supper by quoting a passage from the Belgic Confession. It both teaches a theology of the sacraments and shows how each member of the Trinity is involved in them:

Belgic Confession Q&A 33, in *Reformed Confessions Harmonized*, ed. Joel R. Beeke and Sinclair B. Ferguson (Grand Rapids, MI: Baker, 1999), 208-210.

We believe that our gracious God, on account of our weakness and infirmities, has ordained the sacraments for us, thereby to seal unto us his promises, and to be pledges of the good will and grace of God toward us, and also to nourish and strengthen our faith, which he has joined to the word of the gospel, the better to present to our senses, both that which he s.ignifies to us by his word, and that which he works inwardly in our hearts, thereby assuring and confirming in us the salvation which he imparts to us. For they are visible signs and seals of an inward and invisible thing, by means of which God works in us by the power of the Holy Spirit. Therefore the signs are not in vain or insignificant, so as to deceive us. For Jesus Christ is the true object presented by them, without whom they would be of no moment.

Prayers before or after administering the bread and cup provide another opportunity to underscore the Trinitarian dimensions of the Table. For example, the *Order of the Church in Denmark* (1548) offers a lovely Trinitarian prayer of thanksgiving to follow the Lord's Supper:

Miles Coverdale, "The Order That the Church and Congregation of Christ in Denmark, and in Many Places, Countries and Cities in Germany Do Use, Not Only at the Holy Supper of the Lord, but Also at the Ministration of the Blessed Sacrament of Baptism and Holy Wedlock," in *Reformation Worship: Liturgies from the Past for the Present*, ed. Jonathan Gibson and Mark Earngey (Greensboro, NC: New Growth Press, 2018), 275.

O Lord God Almighty, we thank you with all our hearts that you have fed our souls with the body and blood of your most dear Son. And we sincerely ask you to illuminate our minds with your Holy Spirit, that we may daily increase in strength of faith in you, in certainty of hope in your promises, and earnest love toward you and our neighbours, to the glory and praise of your holy name. Amen.

In sum, local churches should treat baptism and the Lord's Supper as vital parts of their corporate worship. Pastors should devote time to explaining what they mean. The sacraments engage us in communion with the triune God.

I am not commenting here on how often churches should observe the Lord's Supper, since I do not understand Scripture to mandate any particular frequency. It is possible to celebrate the Lord's Supper regularly, though not weekly, and for it to still be a core, vital part of the church's corporate worship.

PRAYER

The prayers of the church provide another crucial avenue for relating to the triune God. Many believers wonder about how to pray to the Trinity. What is the primary training ground where Christians learn to pray? It's the local church.

In union with the Son of God, we cry out to God as Abba, Father, by the Spirit (Rom 8:15). We address God as Spirit-filled adopted children who are fellow heirs with Christ the Son, our mediator (Rom 8:17). To pray "in Jesus' name" means that we pray in line with these Trinitarian realities. In other words, Christian prayer is well described by the common summary statement: we pray *to* the Father, *in and through* the Son, *by* the power of the Holy Spirit. Of course, we may legitimately address each person of the Trinity in prayer, as each is fully divine. It is wise, though, to teach and model corporate prayer that reflects an awareness of how union with Christ informs our engagement with the triune God. Fred Sanders rightly argues that prayer to the Father, through the Son, by the Spirit is "aligned with reality," a way of "praying with the grain" of how God has called us into relationship with him. The point is not constantly to repeat the Trinitarian formula "to... through... by..." in a tedious way, but rather simply to pray, pray, and pray some more, informed by good Trinitarian theology.

Sanders, The Deep Things of God, 220.

From my vantage point in evangelicalism, it seems that a helpful start at highlighting the Trinity in our corporate prayer would simply involve praying more often and more thoughtfully in our church meetings. Paul encourages Timothy to lead his church in "petitions, prayers, intercession and thanksgiving" (1 Tim 2:1); dozens upon dozens of psalms are corporate prayers. But prayer plays a perfunctory role in too many worship services today. It is a mere concluding note to a set of songs, or an introductory transition to a sermon.

For an excellent guide to including such prayers in a church service, see John Onwuchekwa, Prayer: How Praying Together Shapes the Church (Wheaton, IL: Crossway, 2018), 78-89.

By offering substantive prayers of adoration, confession, thanksgiving and supplication, we not only teach people how to pray. We also provide ample opportunity for Trinitarian reflection. Just as faithful song leaders give time and effort to arranging music for the church's corporate singing, and pastors labour diligently to craft a sermon, it is worthwhile for elders to work hard at preparing excellent prayers – ones that are several minutes long rather than 15 seconds, and particularly ones that show an awareness of God's triune nature. This need not mean that prayers be entirely scripted; the point is that corporate prayer itself is a *ministry*, one with great power to lead a congregation to delight in the triune God. A young man at my church recently offered a prayer of praise that included sentences like these: "We praise you that your life abounds in perfection. In eternal fellowship with your Son and Spirit, you have no lack and you know no need... We praise you, Father, that with your exalted Son you poured out the promised Holy Spirit."

Prayer is a double-edged sword in corporate worship. It is both a means by which we commune with the triune God and a teaching tool by which we instruct the congregation, week after week, about who God is.

READING AND PREACHING THE WORD

God the Father presents his Son, the eternal Word, to us in the Spirit-inspired Scripture. When the church hears God's word read and preached, the triune God is at work in her midst. Jesus taught of the Holy Spirit: "He will glorify me because it is from me that he will receive what he will make known to you. All that belongs to the Father is mine. That is why I said the Spirit will receive from me what he will make known to you" (John 16:14-15). The Spirit thus inspired the apostles as he did the Old Testament prophets (2 Pet 1:21). In both eras, the substance of his message was Christ.

It is strange, then, that many churches seem to associate the reading and preaching of Scripture primarily with the act of "learning." For sure, the ministry of the word doesn't result in *less* than learning – but it should involve far *more*. The word is a sharp dagger, Hebrews tells us (4:12). By his word, the triune God convicts, refashions, sanctifies, soothes, and feeds us. When we hear God speak in his word, the Holy Spirit works in us in ways beyond our ability to explain, providing us the rich sustenance of the Saviour. Todd Billings puts it this way:

Billings, *Remembrance, Communion, and Hope*, 25.

...meditation upon God's word, for Christians, inserts them into a triune drama where the Spirit is reshaping God's people into the image of Christ.

Therefore, churches that desire the supernatural ministry of the Holy Spirit should commit themselves to a robust diet of Scripture. The Spirit inspired the word; we honour him by hearing it and submitting to it. He normally ministers to us in and through his word, not separate from it.

Simple words of introduction or conclusion can help a congregation recognise the Trinitarian dimensions of reading and preaching the word. "Now hear the message of Christ, given to us by the Holy Spirit, to the glory of the Father." "God the Father has spoken to us by his Spirit, offering us hope in his Son."

In addition, creeds are an especially useful and historically-rooted way to encapsulate the preaching ministry of the church, and many ancient creeds are richly Trinitarian. My church reads the Apostles' and Nicene Creeds corporately several times each year.

Over the centuries, Christians have written countless hymns that reflect on God's triune nature. These days, though, the Trinity seems absent from much sung praise, except when churches select *Holy, Holy, Holy* or *How Great Is Our God*.

What accounts for this omission? In a fascinating study, Lester Ruth analyses the top 77 "contemporary worship songs" used by churches from 1989 to 2005, as reported by the copyright company CCLI. He observes that very few of these songs reference the Trinity or name the persons of the Godhead, and offers a few possible explanations. First, there is a "lack of theological expectations for the songs;" in an effort to stimulate an emotional response, songwriters have tended to shy away from theology and have instead prioritised "a shared affective experience." Next, there are real forces of supply and demand in play, which influence how publishers market their product – worship songs – to pastors and music leaders.

Lester Ruth, "How Great Is Our God: The Trinity in Contemporary Christian Worship Music," in *The Message in the Music: Studying Contemporary Praise and Worship*, ed. Robert Woods and Brian Walrath (Nashville: Abingdon Press, 2007), 39.

ibid., 41.

Christians within this production and marketing system have not noticed the omission [of the Trinity] because they have valued the songs on other grounds.

Finally, in some churches a theology of intimacy with Christ *through* the medium of music has undermined Christ's role as mediator:

ibid., 43.

If worship's primary end is communion with the Son, not necessarily with God the Father – a communion understood as personal intimacy – the need for Christ as mediator is itself lessened. Mediation is shifted to the music, it appears. Thus prayer in [contemporary worship music] is not primarily to the Father through the Son but to the Son through the music.

How should we respond? To begin, we must insist that sung worship participates in the Trinitarian dynamics discussed earlier. Led by Christ and in union with him, the church sings to the glory of the triune God as those who are a dwelling place for the Spirit. Though certainly not every song must reference these Trinitarian realities nor name the three persons of the Godhead, pastors would do well to audit their canon of songs and determine how often they actually mention or allude to the Trinity.

We also must recover an understanding of singing as part of the ministry of the word. "Let the word of Christ dwell in you richly," Paul instructs, in part by "psalms, hymns, and songs from the Spirit" (Col 3:16). Hymns teach. They shape and disciple believers. It is incumbent on pastors, therefore, to select only the best songs. Our hymns will either help the church know and delight in the Trinity, or they will perpetuate ignorance of God's triune nature.

With that in mind, you've probably noticed that throughout this article I have assumed that pastors (that is, those who bear the office of elder) are responsible for planning corporate services. The elders of the church must be "able to teach" (1 Tim 3:2). Since every element of the worship gathering, including each song, plays a teaching role, it is vital for the elders to exercise oversight over song selection. The musicians can be involved in the process, of course. But pastors must take overall responsibility. What a glorious opportunity: the shepherds of the church each week can lead the people of God to delight in the Father, Son, and Spirit simply through picking excellent Trinitarian songs. Often an old hymnal is a good place to begin looking.

Our corporate worship gatherings are a foretaste of the future. In the new creation, God's people will fellowship with the blessed Trinity forever. What a privilege it is to enjoy a preview of that glorious future each week.

To Fa - ther, Son, and Spi - rit now Our hands we lift, our knees we bow:
To Thee, blest Trin - i - ty, we raise E'en here, in ex - ile, songs of praise.

Questions for further thought and discussion

1. Why not take a few Sundays in the life of your church and do a "Trinity audit" – how transparent would it be to a visitor that your church worships a Trinitarian God?

2. Why does Matt think we don't have to choose between Christ-centred worship and Trinitarian worship?

3. Historically, a wide range of churches celebrate Trinity Sunday every year (in 2020 it will be Sunday 7th June). How could you use this issue of *Primer* to plan to focus more explicitly on the Trinity around that Sunday, or elsewhere in the life of your church?

A Profound Mystery

How the Trinity helps in our evangelism

Most people think that the Trinity will complicate evangelism. We assume that sharing the gospel is easy but explaining the Trinity is hard.

But if you consider the nature of evangelism for a moment, it turns out that it is already a nested set of mysteries in itself: How does a person become a Christian? How can a few sentences in a human conversation bring about salvation, and launch a person on an endless journey into the life of God?

It is precisely here that the Trinity helps. All of these mysteries lead toward, are sorted out by, and culminate in, the mystery of the Trinity. In other words, evangelism is a mystery solved by the Trinity, because evangelism is inescapably Trinitarian. This article, therefore, considers the various ways the mysteries of evangelism already have the Trinity lurking within them.

FRED SANDERS is a systematic theologian who specialises in the doctrine of the Trinity. He teaches at Biola University in the Torrey Honors Institute. He is the author of several books and is a member of Grace Evangelical Free Church.

@FredFredSanders

I.

One mystery that may loom especially large for any evangelist is the surprising contrast between the brief message and the big result. Or (to put the contrast another way) how few words we say when sharing the gospel, versus how vast the reality of salvation is. This mystery is a kind of discrepancy of **scale**: how can a handful of words bring somebody into contact with the personal reality of God's salvation? Already in the New Testament we see striking examples of this contrast. When Matthew tells us (Matt 3:2) that Jesus preached "Repent, for the kingdom of heaven has come near," that very brief message is probably a shorthand summary for Jesus' full message, as expanded in the Sermon on the Mount. Still, it is a strikingly short formula: a nine-word command for response to God's decisive action. When the jailer in Philippi asks Paul, "What must I do to be saved?" he responds with a handful of words: "Believe in the Lord Jesus, and you will be saved – you and your household." Again, these thirteen words reported in Acts 16 are a condensed, introductory summary of the whole message. We are told immediately that Paul and Silas went on and "spoke the word of the Lord to him and to all the others in his house."

Perhaps the most striking New Testament example of a short message producing an outsized evangelistic result is Peter's speech in Acts 10, in the house of Cornelius. "You know the message God sent to the people of Israel," Peter tells these Gentiles. He goes on for a couple of hundred words (about ten verses), explaining clearly how God was "announcing the good news of peace through Jesus Christ," describing the key points in the life and work of Jesus Christ. His story falls very much into the pattern of the second article of the Apostles' Creed. He concludes that "everyone who believes in him receives forgiveness of sins through his name." But perhaps "concludes" is not the right word, because Luke tells us that "While Peter was still speaking these words, the Holy Spirit came on all who heard the message." Surely this is among the greatest interrupted sermons of all time. Something massive broke out there in the house of Cornelius, triggered by Peter's clear account of the saving life of Christ. We can anticipate the Trinitarian aspect of this evangelistic event by saying that when Peter testified about the Son of God, the Spirit of God bore witness to the truth and reality of what he said. The Spirit bore witness to Christ, and salvation came to the house of Cornelius. The persons of the Trinity were in that room. The Spirit made Christ present; though the Son was exalted to the right hand of the Father, he was present in power where salvation was offered in his name.

Anybody who has proclaimed the gospel and seen people respond to it will recognise this pattern. No matter how competently the good news is set forth, the words spoken still amount to a mere handful. The response, when a listener experiences salvation, simply seems all out of proportion. The reason, of course, is that counting words is not the right way to measure spiritual communication. While God consents for his message to be carried along on faithful words (the pattern of which he himself provides by inspiration), that message is not ultimately about the words, but about a spiritual reality. Evangelism is a verbal expression of a more-than-verbal reality, testifying to the presence of something, or rather of someone, who is truly there. The knowledge communicated through evangelism is knowledge by acquaintance rather than knowledge by description. That is why it doesn't have to be an account that is proportionate to the result. Evangelistic words are pointers that indicate, or pick out, the Son by the power of the Spirit.

Evangelism is a verbal expression of a more-than-verbal reality, testifying to the presence of something, or rather of someone, who is truly there.

II.

This brings us to a second mystery, which is not a contrast of scale but of **depth**. Anyone communicating the gospel will necessarily pick out for presentation a few key elements of the message. A wise communicator will select, if possible, truths which are both central to the faith and also well suited for an introduction. What is amazing about proclaiming the Christian message is the way the simple truths, which can be explained and understood briefly by way of introduction, are so immediately connected to the deep truths which nobody will ever get to the bottom of or outgrow. Not many fields of knowledge are like this: we learn to cook by boiling eggs and toasting bread, but move on to advanced techniques and different ingredients. We learn to repair mechanical things by starting on simple machines and moving upward in complexity. The subject matter of geometry expands materially from first principles (point and line and plane) by developing more and more operations; the first pages of a geometry book are almost too simple, but skip forward twenty pages and the complexity is striking. But the Christian message introduces the reality of God the Father sending his Son and his Spirit to atone for our sins and bring us into fellowship, and further pondering of the Christian message only takes inquirers further into these same truths. We might say of salvation what Gregory the Great said about the Bible, that a lamb can wade in it while an elephant can swim.

Again, as with the mystery of scale and proportion, the explanation of this mystery is that the things we come into contact with at the beginning of the Christian life are not simply things (propositions, principles, claims), but spiritual realities. They are ultimately divine persons, the Son and the Spirit sent for our salvation by God the Father. We meet them in the message of salvation and never outgrow them in our spiritual development, because they are, in person, the good news of God's salvation. What we receive, as Paul says in 1 Cor 2:12, is "the Spirit who is from God, so that we may understand what God has freely given us." Notice that the gift of salvation has layers; it is a kind of double gift that includes something given ("what God has freely given us"), and something further given to increase our knowledge of what was given ("the Spirit who is from God, so that we may understand"). This is the spiritual wisdom imparted in salvation and Paul reaches for Trinitarian categories to explain it: God the Father gives believers both his Spirit, who searches all things (1 Cor 2:10-12), and knowledge of the mind of the Lord by way of the mind of Christ (1 Cor 2:16).

Here we see the Trinitarian reality underlying any person coming to faith. The God of the Christian faith is triune; Father, Son, and Spirit. But the structure of Christian faith itself is Trinitarian, mediated in us by the light of Christ and the witness of the Spirit. And that means that our way of understanding is correspondingly threefold, as we grow by coming to greater knowledge of the Father through the mind of Christ and the searching of the Spirit.

A responsible evangelist will carefully select which parts of the total Christian message to communicate first, just as any communicator on any subject would. In fact, the actual doctrine of the Trinity (three persons in one being, how they are related to each other, and so on) might not be among the first topics to be broached. But the mystery of Trinitarian depth means that in evangelism there is a peculiar kind of levelling effect, wherein the first truths are also the final truths. The most seasoned and profound spiritual thinkers will admit that they are only sinking deeper into the very realities that they encountered when they first believed. J. I. Packer put the point this way, after having explained salvation at some length: "Christ is what he is to believers... irrespective of how much or how little of this multiple relationship they have with him is clear to their minds." And he recognised the similarity between the profoundest thinker and the new believer:

...the first truths are also the final truths.

J. I. Packer, *Keep in Step with the Spirit* (Leicester: IVP, 1984), 42.

Packer, *Keep in Step with the Spirit*, 42.

An apostolic theologian like Paul, for instance, had it all far clearer in his mind than did the penitent thief of Luke 23:39-43; yet Jesus' saving ministry was as rich to the one as to the other, and we may be sure that at this very moment the two of them, the apostle and the bandit, are together before the throne, their differences in theological expertise on earth making no difference whatsoever to their enjoyment of Christ in heaven.

The Puritans distinguished between union and communion: union with Christ was an underlying reality that was the same for all Christians; while communion was an experience of fellowship that varied among believers and even throughout the course of one's life. "Union is the foundation of communion," said Richard Sibbes. Communion arises from union, and seeks a fuller realisation of it. The mystery of depth lies here, in the way that even the greatest spiritual growth consists in greater realisation, experience, and understanding of, the union all believers share in the Trinity. All believers have, by nature, union with the Trinity; through spiritual experience and theological growth we cultivate communion with the Trinity.

Sibbes' book has a long and difficult original title but is usually referred to as "Sibbes on Union and Communion." See *The Complete Works of Richard Sibbes*, vol II (Edinburgh: James Nichol, 1862), 174.

III.

These mysteries of scale and depth bring us to the third mystery, which is a mystery of **agency**. When we are astonished that the human action of evangelism can bring about the divine result of salvation, we are registering the fact that the human action of evangelism is not the whole story. The words in which the gospel is communicated are human words with divine testimony in them, and the divine testimony is what is doing the work. The great Reformed theologian Zacharius Ursinus pointed out that since "conversion is the gift of God alone," it would be madness "to attribute this conversion to the efficacy of man's voice." And yet it pleases God to bring about conversion by the "foolishness of preaching," a phrase in which Ursinus seems to hear the radical disproportion between human words and divine effects in evangelism.

Ursinus, "Hortatory Oration to the Study of Divinity," in *The Summe of Christian Religion* (London, 1645), 6.

When the New Testament underscores this mystery of agency, it tends to break into Trinitarian terms and patterns. Consider Luke 10, when the disciples report to Jesus that some towns have accepted his message while others have not:

Luke 10:21-22

> At that time Jesus, full of joy through the Holy Spirit, said, "I praise you, Father, Lord of heaven and earth, because you have hidden these things from the wise and learned, and revealed them to little children. Yes, Father, for this is what you were pleased to do. All things have been committed to me by my Father. No one knows who the Son is except the Father, and no one knows who the Father is except the Son and those to whom the Son chooses to reveal him."

> **The only way into this closed circle of divine knowledge is by the Son's revelation of the Father.**

Jesus the Son, rejoicing in the Holy Spirit, thanks the Father for sovereignly revealing his truth to the simple while concealing it from the learned. As Jesus goes on to say, the knowledge of God is something locked up inside of God himself, and only by revelation is it made known to human persons. But Jesus puts this in interpersonal terms, saying not simply that "God knows himself," but that the Son knows the Father, and the Father knows the Son. The only way into this closed circle of divine knowledge is by the Son's revelation of the Father. In another place, Jesus not only points to his Father as the one who reveals, but explicitly contrasts the Father's work with human agency: "this was not revealed to you by flesh and blood, but by my Father in heaven." (Matt 16:17)

IV.

These lesser mysteries of evangelism all lead up to **the great mystery of the Trinity.** Indeed, it was impossible to explore these mysteries of scale, depth, and agency without falling into the triple cadence of Trinitarian theology: the Spirit bearing witness to the Son; the Son revealing the Father; the Father having sent the Son and the Spirit for this very purpose. Salvation is an encounter with the Trinity, bringing about knowledge of the Trinity, through the effective work of the Trinity. The gospel is the good news of salvation worked out by the Father, Son, and Holy Spirit.

But even when these Trinitarian depths of the gospel are recognised, it is still worth asking whether the doctrine of the Trinity needs to be made explicitly a part of the message in evangelism. Do we need to speak about the triunity of God when introducing people to the Christian faith? As a matter of technique, arguments could be made for holding off on it, or for diving right in. Obviously it's a complex sounding doctrine, which could be distracting. People who are vaguely aware of the doctrine may also associate it with irrationality, on the assumption that it teaches a contradiction. This objection can be met readily enough, but the argument itself is likely to lead a conversation further afield from gospel issues. So then, there is a good case to be made for postponing mention of the Trinity in evangelism.

On the other hand, inquirers need to be told about this doctrine fairly early, or they may feel cheated later, as if they'd been invited into the faith on the grounds of forgiveness but then were shocked to learn that they had to swallow a difficult doctrine of God. Furthermore, there may be advantages to sharing this unusual-sounding doctrine earlier. Mightn't the sheer oddness of it be rather compelling for a modern audience? Doesn't it have just the right amount of peculiarity to it, the kind of peculiarity that marks the unpredictable reality of scientific puzzles? And if you are sharing the Christian message with a more intellectual acquaintance, isn't there something helpful about having a really tough doctrine to ponder?

But these concerns are all in danger of bottoming out at the level of mere technique. They are not substantially different from the kind of calculations any salesman would make in communicating their message about insurance, pest removal, or costly repairs. The mystery of the Trinity points in another direction entirely: it points to the gospel as God's own self-giving for our salvation. The good news that the Father sent the Son and the Spirit means that God did not delegate salvation, or carry it out by remote control, but came to be among us personally, historically, concretely. If anything calls us away from evangelism as mere technique, in danger of manipulation, it is a clear view of the Trinitarian nature of God. Because the message of salvation is that God the Father so loved the world that he sent his Son, and that nobody can call Jesus "Lord" except by the Holy Spirit, who was given to us so that we might understand what God has freely given.

In light of the Trinitarian depth of evangelism, it's no surprise that the key New Testament passages about evangelism are prominent passages about the three persons of the Trinity. Consider Matt 28:18-20: Jesus commissions his disciples to "go and make disciples of all nations, baptising them in the name of the Father and of the Son and of the Holy Spirit, and teaching them to obey everything I have commanded you." The sending out of the disciples happens on the basis of the Son's glorification by the Father and the Spirit. Similarly, in the language of John's Gospel, the risen Christ gives the Trinitarian command, "As the Father has sent me, I am sending you," and then breathes on them and says, "Receive the Holy Spirit." (John 20:21-22) *Sending* verses tend to be *Trinity* verses. That is because Christian mission is the result of the Trinity's own mission.

...Christian mission is the result of the Trinity's own mission.

In passages like this, the biblical authors are not setting out primarily to teach the doctrine of God. Instead, what they are manifestly teaching about is the nature of salvation, and doing so in the context of mission and evangelism. But along the way, they necessarily include teaching about the God of that salvation, precisely in the form of references to the Son and the Spirit as sent from the Father. The close connection between salvation passages and Trinity passages is no mere coincidence. It arises from the fact that the Trinity and salvation belong together. The lesson this suggests is that while we don't always have to talk about the doctrine of the Trinity in our evangelism, we do have to pay attention to the presence of God the Trinity in evangelism. Our evangelism is an extension of how the Trinity does evangelism.

In his 1665 book *Heaven Opened*, Richard Alleine made "A Brief and Plain Discovery of the Riches of God's Covenant of Grace." Alleine announced the covenant of grace as "good news indeed," and asked, what is the content of the covenant that God had granted? What is in God's plan of salvation? "In sum," he said, "there is all that heaven and earth can afford; all that can be needed or desired; and this, by a firm and irrevocable deed, made over, and made sure to all that will sincerely embrace it." In God's salvation we have three main things: God himself, God's own Son, and God's own Spirit. This encounter with God in his gospel is the blessing of salvation, and the proclamation of that good news never happens without the Trinity. It always happens within the Trinity.

Richard Alleine, *Heaven Opened, Or a Brief and Plain Discovery of the Riches of God's Covenant of Grace* (New York: American Tract Society, 1852), 8.

Questions for further thought and discussion

1. How does this article, and this issue of *Primer* as a whole, help us see that the gospel of salvation is bound up with the persons of the Trinity in a very close way? By now this should take a while to answer ;-)

2. Fred says that a grasp of the Trinity focusses the gospel on "God's own self-giving for our salvation." How might that help our evangelism in a culture suspicious of power and manipulation? And how might it challenge a culture which is so desperately self-obsessed?